Speaking Code

Software Studies
Matthew Fuller, Lev Manovich, and Noah Wardrip-Fruin, editors

Expressive Processing: Digital Fictions, Computer Games, and Software Studies,
Noah Wardrip-Fruin, 2009

Code/Space: Software and Everyday Life,
Rob Kitchin and Martin Dodge, 2011

Programmed Visions: Software and Memory,
Wendy Hui Kyong Chun, 2011

Speaking Code: Coding as Aesthetic and Political Expression,
text: Geoff Cox; code: Alex McLean, 2012

Speaking Code

Coding as Aesthetic and Political Expression

text: Geoff Cox

code: Alex McLean

foreword by Franco "Bifo" Berardi

The MIT Press
Cambridge, Massachusetts
London, England

MIT Press books may be purchased at special quantity discounts for business or sales promotional use. For information, please email special_sales@mitpress.mit.edu or write to Special Sales Department, The MIT Press, 55 Hayward Street, Cambridge, MA 02142.

This book was set in Stone Sans and Stone Serif by Toppan Best-set Premedia Limited. Printed and bound in the United States of America.

Library of Congress Cataloging-in-Publication Data

Cox, Geoff.
Speaking code : coding as aesthetic and political expression / text [by] Geoff Cox, code [by] Alex McLean, foreword by Franco "Bifo" Berardi.
    p. cm.—(Software studies)
Includes bibliographical references and index.
ISBN 978-0-262-01836-4 (hardcover : alk. paper)
1. Source code (Computer science)—Philosophy. 2. Programming languages (Electronic computers)—Syntax. 3. Computer prose. I. McLean, Alex (Christopher Alex), 1975– II. Title.
QA76.167.C69   2013
005.1—dc23
2012012944

10 9 8 7 6 5 4 3 2 1

Contents

Series Foreword

Software is deeply woven into contemporary life—economically, culturally, creatively, politically—in manners both obvious and nearly invisible. Yet while much is written about how software is used, and the activities that it supports and shapes, thinking about software itself has remained largely technical for much of its history. Increasingly, however, artists, scientists, engineers, hackers, designers, and scholars in the humanities and social sciences are finding that for the questions they face, and the things they need to build, an expanded understanding of software is necessary. For such understanding they can call upon a strand of texts in the history of computing and new media, they can take part in the rich implicit culture of software, and they also can take part in the development of an emerging, fundamentally transdisciplinary, computational literacy. These provide the foundation for Software Studies.

Software Studies uses and develops cultural, theoretical, and practice-oriented approaches to make critical, historical, and experimental accounts of (and interventions via) the objects and processes of software. The field engages and contributes to the research of computer scientists, the work of software designers and engineers, and the creations of software artists. It tracks how software is substantially integrated into the processes of contemporary culture and society, reformulating processes, ideas, institutions, and cultural objects around their closeness to algorithmic and formal description and action. Software Studies proposes histories of computational cultures and works with the intellectual resources of computing to develop reflexive thinking about its entanglements and possibilities. It does this both in the scholarly modes of the humanities and social sciences and in the software creation/research modes of computer science, the arts, and design.

The Software Studies book series, published by the MIT Press, aims to publish the best new work in a critical and experimental field that is at once culturally and technically literate, reflecting the reality of today's software culture.

Foreword: Debt, Exactness, Excess

Franco "Bifo" Berardi

Pragmatics, or the future of language

Language and the future: this is the subject of this book. Not the rhetorical future of history, politics, and so on, but the pragmatic future of the next second, of the next minute, of the next action and interaction. Future and interaction: this is the task (or the destiny) of code. So code is "speaking" us. Geoff Cox is trying to show the other side of the moon: if we can say that code is speaking us (pervading and formatting our action), the other way round is also true. We are speaking code in many ways. In the beginning someone is writing the code, and others are supposed to submit themselves to the effects of the code written by someone. Power is more and more inscribed in code. Writing to Thomas Sebeok, Bill Gates once remarked that "power is making things easy" (quoted by Arthur Kroker and Michael A. Weinstein in *Data Trash*, 1994). Code and interfaces: interfaces are supposed to make the complexity of the code easy, but code in itself is more often about simplifying technical procedures of social life, particularly of economic production and exchange. So code is speaking us, but we are not always working through the effects of written code. More and more we are escaping (or trying to escape) the automatisms implied in the written code.

Prescriptions, prophecies, injunctions are ways of inscribing the future in language, and—most importantly—are ways of producing the future by means of language. Like prescriptions, prophecies, and injunctions, code also has the power to inscribe the future, by formatting linguistic relations and the pragmatic development of algorithmic signs. Code is modeling the future, as the future is inscribed in code. In fact the implementation of code is performing our environment, our behavior. Code is prescribing what we will do to the machine and what the machine will do to us. Financial code, for instance, is triggering a series of linguistic automatisms that are able to model and perform social activity, consumption patterns and lifestyles. Algorithms are numeric combinations that inscribe in themselves operational functions, formatting and performing the real developments of the human world.

But the pragmatic effects of the code are not deterministic, as far as the code is the product of code writing, and code writing is affected by social, political, cultural, and emotional processes. This is a key point that is highlighted in this book. Hacking, free software, WikiLeaks . . . are the names of lines of escape from the determinism of code.

From this point of view, *Speaking Code* is a timely intervention. It again raises the question of pragmatics previously debated by authors like J. L. Austin (*How to Do Things with Words*, 1962), Paul Watzlawick (*Pragmatics of Human Communication*, 1967), and Félix Guattari (*L'inconscient machinique*, 1979), but in this book, for the first time, the problem of pragmatics is investigated at the level of code. The pragmatics of code is opening the door to a flow of urgent questions directly coming from the field of current events and present history. Think of the financial crisis and the tremendous social effects it is provoking: if we want to understand something about this crisis that is haunting Western politics and daily life we have to focus on the pragmatics of code.

According to Robert J. Sardello, in *Money and the Soul of the World* (1983), money and language have something in common: they are nothing and yet affect everything. They are nothing but symbols, conventions, *flatus vocis*, but they have the power of persuading human beings to act, to work, and to transform physical things. "Money makes things happen. It is the source of action in the world and perhaps the only power we invest in. Perhaps in every other respect, in every other value, bankruptcy has been declared, giving money the power of some sacred deity, demanding to be recognized." Language is nothing, like money. But like money, language can do anything, up to the point that, as Martin Heidegger suggests, "what we know of Being is what can be elaborated by Language." Language and money are shaping our future in many ways. Like prophecy.

Prophecy is a form of prediction that is able to act on the development of the future thanks to the effect of persuasion, emotionality, and pervasion of the audience. Thanks to the social effects of psychological reactions to language, prophecy can act in a self-fulfilling way. The financial economy is marked by self-fulfilling prophecies. When rating agencies downgrade the value of an enterprise, or national economy, what they make is a prediction about the future performances of the enterprise, or economy. But this prediction is heavily influencing the actors of the economic game, so much so that the downgrading results in an actual loss of reliability and an actual loss of economic value. So the prophecy comes true. How can we escape the effects of prophecy? How can we escape the effects of code? Of course these are two different problems, but they have very much in common.

The limits of language

In his latest book (*E così via, all'infinito*, 2010) Paolo Virno again questions the problem of the limits of language. Rereading Ludwig Wittgenstein's assertion that the limits of my language are the limits of my world, Virno looks for a means of escape from the determinist effects of the implied limitations of language. The linguistic excess, namely poetry, art, and desire, are conditions for the overcoming and the displacement of the limits that linguistic practice presupposes.

In the preface to his *Tractatus Logico-Philosophicus* (1922), Wittgenstein writes: "In order to draw a limit to thinking we should have to be able to think both sides of this limit (we should therefore have to be able to think what cannot be thought)." And he writes: "The limits of my language are the limits of my world. Logic pervades the world: the limits of the world are also its limits. So we cannot say in logic, 'The world has this in it, and this, but not that.' For that would appear to presuppose that we were excluding certain possibilities, and this cannot be the case, since it would require that logic should go beyond the limits of the world; for only in that way could it view those limits from the other side as well. We cannot think what we cannot think; so what we cannot think we cannot say either." And finally he writes: "The subject does not belong to the world: rather, it is a limit of the world."

When Wittgenstein says that the limits of language are the limits of the world, we should read this in two different ways. First he is saying: what we cannot say we cannot do, we cannot experience, we cannot live, as only in the sphere of language can we interact with the reality of Being. But he is also saying: as the world is what resides inside the limits of our language, therefore beyond the limits of language lies what we will be able to live and experience only when our language will be able to elaborate that sphere of Being that lies beyond the present limit. In fact he writes: "The subject does not belong to the world, rather it is a limit of the world." The potency and extension of language depends on the consistency of the subject, on its vision, on its situation. And the extension of my world depends on the potency of my language.

The process of going beyond the limits of the world is what Guattari calls "chaosmosis," and he refers to this going beyond as "re-semiotization," i.e., the redefinition of the semiotic limit, which is also the limit of the experience of the world. Scientists call this effect of autopoietic morphogenesis "emergence": a new form comes out and takes shape when logical-linguistic conditions make it possible to see it, and to name it. Let's try to understand our present situation from this point of view.

Digital financial capitalism has created a closed reality, which cannot be overcome with the technicalities of politics, of consciously organized voluntary action and of government. Only an act of language may give us the possibility of seeing and of creating a new human condition where now we only see barbarianism and violence. Only an act of language escaping the technical automatisms of financial capitalism will make possible the emergence of a new life form. The new form of life will be the social and desiring body of the general intellect, the social and desiring body that the general intellect is deprived of, under the present conditions of financial dictatorship. Only the reactivation of the body of the general intellect—the organic, existential, historical finitude that is bringing in itself the potency of the general intellect—will be able to imagine new infinities. Only in the intersection of the finite and infinite, in the point of negotiation between complexity and chaos, will it be possible to disentangle degrees of complexity higher than that which financial capitalism is able to manage and elaborate.

Language is an infinite potency, but the exercise of language happens in finite conditions of history and existence. Thanks to the establishment of such a limit, the world comes to exist as a world of language. Grammar, logic, ethics are all based on the institution of a limit. Code is a limited exercise of language and simultaneously it is the institution of a (performing and productive) limit. Limits can be productive, but outside of this limited space the infinite possibilities of language persist immeasurably.

Code implies syntactic exactness of linguistic signs: connection. Compatibility and consistency and syntactic exactness are the conditions of operational functionality of code. Proprietary code is language in debt. Only exacting the necessary syntactic consistency, language can perform its connective purpose. The excess is the *remise en question* of the infinity of language, the breakdown of consistency, the reopening of the horizon of possibility. Excess is playing the game of conjunction (round bodies looking for meaning out of any syntactic exactness), not the preformatted game of segmental connection.

Poetry is the reopening of the in-definite, the ironic act of exceeding the established meaning of words. In every sphere of human action, grammar is the establishment of limits defining a space of communication. The economy is the universal grammar traversing the different level of human activity nowadays. Also language is defined and limited by its economic exchangeability: in the reduction of language to information, and incorporation of techno-linguistic automatisms in the social circulation of language. Nevertheless, whereas social communication is a limited process, language is boundless: its potentiality is not limited to the limits of the signified. Poetry is the excess of language, the signifier disentangled from the limits of the signified. Irony, the ethical form of the exceeding power of language, is the infinite game that words are playing to create and to skip and to shuffle meanings. Social movements, at the end of the day, can be viewed as ironic acts of language, as semiotic insolvency, as the disentanglement of language, behavior, and action from the limits of symbolic debt. In this book a question is raised: is it possible to speak of code as a movement, as a form of subversion and of redefinition of the limits of language?

Preface

The interplay of text and code that runs through this book underlines the principle that speech says what it will do and does it. Two voices are evident in its pages: one that tends toward the tradition of critical writing in the arts and humanities, and another that derives more from the tradition of computing and software development. Together they interweave through the chapters, formulating arguments that aim to undermine the distinctions between criticism and practice, and that emphasize the aesthetic and political implications of software studies. A collaborative process lies at the heart of this, one that oscillates between expressive and formal conventions of writing. All the same, one can broadly generalize that the text has been written by myself (with the exception of chapter 1, which is co-written) and the code by Alex McLean (although again there are some exceptions). To separate these may help to identify the voices of the work, but the distinction itself should be underplayed between the authors, and even more importantly between the modes of expression in use and the subject disciplines that are invoked. The combinatory aspect also indicates the central importance of the writing subject in meaning production and registers code as an active agent in the process, which further complicates any reductive tendencies in human and machine reading and its interpretation. The cultural meanings generated are understood not as derived from intentionality or source code as such, but from the complex interplay of forces involved in the encoding and decoding of texts and programs.

Consequently the book's ideas are hard to trace or attribute with any certainty. However, it should be acknowledged that some of the chapters rework aspects of previous publications and talks, as well as previous conversations with students and colleagues at Aarhus University, the University of Plymouth, and Transart Institute, where I have been working in recent years. I have tried to indicate these where they are overt, but the ideas inevitably derive from various other outputs in complex and even unknown ways. This reflects the ways that all ideas are borrowed in some sense, and also reflects the normalization of montage techniques that are somewhat prescribed when using a computer to write. With this in mind, I should acknowledge that throughout the early chapters there is also a faint echo of my PhD thesis, "Antithesis: The Dialectics of Software Art," submitted in 2006 to the University of Plymouth and published by the Digital Aesthetics Research group at Aarhus University in 2010. More specifically, and also cited in endnotes, chapter 1 makes reference to previous collaborative essays with Alex McLean and Adrian Ward, "The Aesthetics of Generative Code" (2000) and "Coding Praxis" (2004). Chapter 2 contains some reworking of the unpublished paper "Software Art Has No History," presented at re:place, Second International Conference on the Histories of Media, Art, Science and Technology, Haus der Kulturen der Welt, Berlin (2007); as well as drawing on ideas from "Means-End of Software," in *Interface Criticism*, edited by Christian Ulrik Andersen and Søren Bro Pold (written in 2007, published by Aarhus University Press, 2011). Chapter 3 further draws upon writings produced in support of projects that I have commissioned for Arnolfini, a contemporary arts center in Bristol, UK, as part of my role there as associate curator of online projects, including "Antisocial Notworking" and "Democracy 2.0," as well as a recent related paper, "Virtual Suicide as Decisive Political Act," in *Activist Media and Biopolitics*, edited by Wolfgang Sützl and Theo Hug (University of Innsbruck Press, 2011). Chapter 4 shares some references with "Not Just for Fun," co-written with Alex McLean for the forthcoming book *Fun and Software*, edited by Olga Goriunova, and my short introduction to David Link's *Machine Heart/Das Herz der Maschine* for the "100 Notes—100 Thoughts" series published in connection with dOCUMENTA (13) (Hatje Cantz, 2011). I hope the fact that many of the texts relate to art projects that I have had an active part in developing (through my occasional curatorial work at Arnolfini) helps to assert one of the central principles of the book, namely that coding practices produce significant aesthetic and political effects.

It has already been stated that the majority of the code examples have been provided by Alex McLean, who at the time of writing was completing his PhD thesis entitled "Artist-Programmers and Programming Languages for the Arts" (submitted October 2011), Goldsmiths, University of London. His research includes an investigation into embodied approaches to text-based music within the broad frame of live coding, and so informs many of the ideas in the book, both implicitly and explicitly.

Finally, and not least, I would like to thank the following people who have helped in the formulation of ideas: Christian Ulrik Andersen, Roy Ascott, Tatiana Bazzichelli, Stuart Brisley, Andreas Broeckmann, Sean Cubitt, Matthew Fuller, Rui Guerra, Robert Jackson, Joasia Krysa, Les Liens Invisibles, Søren Bro Pold, Hugo de Rijke, Victoria de Rijke, Adrian Ward; and especially Franco "Bifo" Berardi for his foreword to the book. The anonymous reviewers of the first draft, and Matthew Abbate, Katie Helke Dokshina, Doug Sery, and others at the MIT Press, have also provided excellent advice throughout the process. Significant writing time has been made possible with support from the Center for Digital Urban Living (the Danish Council for Strategic Research, grant 09-063245) and by Aarhus University's interdisciplinary research center Participatory IT, PIT. At a time when education and research activity are under attack by market forces, I am mindful that I have been working on the book in a country that still maintains that education should be free, and yet paradoxically has recently outlawed the existence of "free universities" (by this, I refer to autonomous institutions that call themselves universities). Such contradictions continue to underpin ideas of freedom of expression and the ongoing precarious conditions for the production and distribution of text and code.

For those interested, downloads, further notes, and ongoing discussion can be found at http://www.speaking-code.net.

Geoff Cox
Aarhus, Autumn 2011

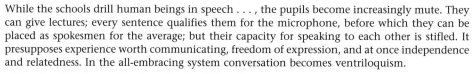

While the schools drill human beings in speech . . . , the pupils become increasingly mute. They can give lectures; every sentence qualifies them for the microphone, before which they can be placed as spokesmen for the average; but their capacity for speaking to each other is stifled. It presupposes experience worth communicating, freedom of expression, and at once independence and relatedness. In the all-embracing system conversation becomes ventriloquism.

—Theodor W. Adorno, "Institute for Deaf-Mutes"

0 Double Coding

```
#!/usr/bin/befunge
>                       v
The  book begins  by  announcing  itself    recursively.  In stating  the
phrasev"Hello World!"<it follows  the   convention that  programmers  adopt
whenv:<learning a new language. The    paragraph executes  itself  in  a  way
that# encapsulates  the   inherent    action  of  code, and  the  central
importance  that will be   developed   around  speech  acts  in  the world.
  v:,_@
  >  ^
```

Using the Befunge programming language to render a first paragraph like this sets the tone for the book in not just describing code and what it does but doing it. As an esoteric language, Befunge also breaks with the conventions of downward direction of interpretation through two-dimensional syntax.[1] This is done using punctuation, with each of the four instructions "∧>∨<" represented by graphical arrows, which change the direction of control flow. "@" ends the program.

The book begins with the "hello world" convention[2] to highlight the ubiquity of speech in everyday communications and the paradoxical tendency seemingly to diminish the power of the voice. Humans and machines increasingly converse with other humans and machines, making our languages ever more codified, but the meanings produced through them are ever more prone to misunderstanding—in the confused spaces between the encoding and decoding of the utterance. Such combinations of natural and artificial languages demonstrate a multilingual human-machine confusion of tongues, under the conditions of contemporary capitalism that have integrated language, intellect, and affect into production.

If in the beginning was the spoken word,[3] this appears to denote the human condition in the breath or essence of life. Underpinning this is the commonly held belief that the soul is the source of speech, which has been forever perverted through the use of spoken language. In the book of Genesis, the world was understood originally to contain one language only—the single language of Adam who first named objects in the world. The story unfolds that the Tower of Babel, designed to reach into heaven, displeased God so much that he (sic) decided to "confound the language of all the earth."[4] Subsequently, everyone has been left to babble in a diversity of languages and confusion of human-machine "tongues," or in new hybrid forms that combine the formal structures of natural languages and program code. These constitute the contemporary babble of communications technologies[5]—resonant in the naming of the contemporary social media platform Twitter with its reductive register of up to 140 characters (condemning everyone to communicate in what is pejoratively called "twitspeak").[6]

Esoteric languages like Befunge, which introduced this chapter, seem to point in another direction altogether, opening up a more indeterminate and expressive space and transcending the production of simple effects or predetermined actions. Take, for another instance, the confounding effects of the esoteric Brainfuck programming language, which offers a challenge to normative source code interpretation by consisting entirely of punctuation, with each of the eight characters "><+-.,[]" representing a single elementary operation. "Hello world!" is expressed thus:

```
>+++++++++[<++++++++>-]<.>+++++++[<++++>-]<+.+++++++..+++.>>>++++++++[<++++>-
]<.>>>++++++++++[<++++++++++>-]<---.<<<<.+++.------.--------.>>+.
```

Taking this indeterminacy further still, Brainfuck exceeds the world of computation in Bodyfuck, an interpreter using computer vision techniques to map bodily gestures to the Brainfuck instruction set.[7]

But as with all signifying systems, interpretation still takes place at all levels, even when they are as esoteric as the examples mentioned above. The reader, whether human or machine, is also cast as one of the objects of the software and operating system. The point can be demonstrated with writing more generally as, in word-processing a text (like this), the writer is also processed into the choice of software and operating system that prescribes or allows certain tasks. It was in recognition of this issue that Friedrich Kittler apologized for his choice of software used to write the essay "There Is No Software."[8] The fact that the user's thoughts and actions are somewhat determined by the operating system or graphical user interface recalls the ways the user is interpellated in the Althusserian sense to demonstrate how ideology calls us to order through its God-like commands and procedures.[9]

This follows an understanding of code in a broad sense, insofar as it can be traced back to its etymological roots through "codicilla" (tablets used for inscribing letter forms) and "codex" (the bound book of the law), as Kittler explains in his entry to the *Software Studies* lexicon.[10] For Kittler, the references establish how code can be understood through the twin operations of command and control.[11] But in addition, and the concern of this book, are the ways in which code also produces ambiguities and possibilities of recoding its prescriptive and deterministic tendencies (the unwritten laws, so to speak). Although instructional, program code cannot simply be reduced to its functional aspects, as it also extends the instability already inherent to the relationship of speech to writing, where it can also go out of control. Like all codes, it is only really interpretable within the context of the overall network of relations that make its operations inherently unstable. It is both a computer-readable notation of logic and a representation of this process, both script and performance; and in this sense it is like spoken words (made explicit in the case of a "hello world" program). It functions in relation to other programs that are simultaneously running in the form of processes that include storage and execution, operating across hardware and software platforms.[12] Indeed, code cannot be separated from the broader systemic framework and the way the technology that inscribes it is embedded in wider processes of command and control.

Coding subject

The common declaration "Hello world" *interpellates* in this way too, not least in the dogged insistence on the use of English as the default "mother tongue" of program languages. To Louis Althusser, the speech act constitutes the subject; it recruits subjects by hailing them, "Hey, you there!," as a policeman (sic) might speak to a passerby.[13] Through the act of recognition the subject begins to exist in ideology, in parallel to the way that program code can be seen to exist in ideology too.

In the following example, the program creates a list of numbers, one of which is made to represent the user of the program. The numbers are arbitrarily connected in a graph structure which is visualized for the user, along with the phrase "Hey, you there." An explicit command like this can be seen to reflect the capacity of programs to authoritatively "speak" to subjects, thus occupying the combined realms of subjectivity and sociality. It is in this sense that speech, or having a voice, connects with political expression and allows for a wider understanding of power relations. However, a more complex articulation of interpellation is required than an emphasis on the determining role of communication systems, as neither the human subject nor program code is quite that passive. Like the historical subject who is interpellated to act in a way that is preordained but not fully known, speech is also retroactive: it is speech in-itself, or speech that preexists itself, "speech before speech," as Slavoj Žižek explains.[14] Things are decided before they are enacted in actuality, and in this sense are always ready to be executed.

```
example@speakingcode:code$ cat | perl
use Graph::Easy;
my $g = Graph::Easy->new();

@ids = (0 .. 15);
$ids[rand(@ids)] = 'you';
foreach $id (0 .. $#ids) {
    $to = rand(@ids) - 1;
    $to++ if ($to >= $id);
    $g->add_edge($ids[$id], $ids[$to]);
}
print($g->as_ascii . "Hey, you there.\n");
```

```
                           +---------------------+
                           v                     |
        +----+         +----+         +-----+         +----+
        | 10 |  -->  | 11 |  -->  |  4  |  -->  | 0  |
        +----+         +----+         +-----+         +----+
                           ^
                           +---------------------+
                                                 |
+---+         +----+         +----+         +-----+         +----+
| 2 | -+  | 8  |  -->  |    |  -->  | you |  -->  | 9  |
+---+ |    +----+         |    |    +-----+         +----+
      |                    |    |       ^
      +----------->  | 15 |       |
                          |    |       |
        +----+        |    |       |              +----+
        | 13 |        |    |  <----+-------- | 12 |
        +----+        +----+       |              +----+
          |                         |
          |                         |
          v                         |
        +----+        +----+        +-----+
        | 14 |  -->  | 6  |  -->  |  3  |
        +----+        +----+        +-----+
                          ^
                          |
                          |
        +----+        +----+
        | 5  |        | 7  |
        +----+        +----+
```

Hey, you there.

Judith Butler also addresses this in her book *Excitable Speech*, drawing attention to the ways in which speech demonstrates agency, as there is a relation between speech and action, between saying and doing.[15] Spoken words say something and do something, and this has consequences in the world, such as in the way insults exert a form of violence. As linguistic beings we are bound to language as part of the constitution of subjectivity (as Althusser described it), so the call to order starts as a form of insult, and we enter into language antagonistically. Speech announces the action that will follow along with this antagonism, hence its power, but also importantly speech sometimes fails or is bounced back through various attempts to resist its determining effects. A good example of this is found in Mladen Dolar's book *A Voice and Nothing More*, which begins with a description of a failure of the voice to interpellate.[16] A command is given loud and clear by a commander of an army to attack its enemy, but nobody acts. The command is repeated over and over again to no effect, until someone says, "What a beautiful voice!" Refusing to execute the command, the soldiers instead contemplate the aesthetic properties of the spoken expression (the soldiers are Italian and perhaps it is their love of opera that informs their actions, rather than pacifism or fear of dying). The speculation is that esoteric languages similarly shift attention from command and control toward cultural expression and refusal.

Moreover, there is a well-established paradox in such a straightforward view of agency derived from the Althusserian concept of interpellation, with its stress on the determining role of language. If the subject is to some extent constituted in language and code, then to think that someone saying and doing something is a straightforward demonstration of agency misses the point; language and code constituted them in the first place, and as such the formation of the human subject is always an unfinished project. Interpellation seems to be bound up in contradiction in this respect, poised between the subject that speaks and the subject that is constituted through speech. If subjects are constituted in language in this paradoxical way, it follows that they also have the ability to reconstitute themselves through language, and even reconstitute the institution of language itself. Clearly there are other possibilities of agency operating outside the "sovereign autonomy of speech," and this is what Butler refers to as "excitable" states. Her assertion is that "speech is always in some ways out of control."[17]

Put differently, speech is far more distributed and networked than simply emanating from a single body, and the call to order is rather more like being allocated an Internet protocol (IP) address that defines you as a unique user in the network (and the example of code at the end of this chapter tries to demonstrate this point).[18] This also serves to emphasize the social aspect of speech—in that language itself is social and in speaking there is always an "echo of others in the act of speech," as Butler puts it.[19] Moreover, it is not that interpellation doesn't occur but that it operates in ever more subtle ways across complex informational networks, along with the networked forms of subjectivity it partly constitutes. This is what Brian Holmes refers to as the "double constitution of the subject," generating both machine-like humans and human-like machines, conjoined through closed-loop informational systems.[20] Indeed, computer programs interpellate through the dual registers of command and control—and they do this at multiple levels of operation, and they also tend toward an executable logic that appears predetermined and unchangeable. Yet the program was programmed in the first place. So although on the surface program code appears to operate in a similar sovereign manner with straightforward agency, namely a command to execute an instruction from sovereign code, the argument that unfolds through this book is that in significant ways these operations are also prone to bugs and failure, and in significant ways can be considered to be out of control, like speech.

Although the analogy between program code and speech acts has become rather commonplace since its suggestion by Terry Winogrand and Fernando Flores in 1987,[21] the stress here is on the degree of indeterminacy they share, as with the example of live coding, where the writing of the software happens at the same time as performing with the software.[22] Programmers express themselves through the use of program languages, the book suggests, in ways similar to other human communicative expression through language and gesture. They do this through their manipulation of layers of representation, including symbols, then words, language, and notation, as exemplified in the production of software prototypes, artworks, programming languages, and improvised performances that embed the activity of programming in the improvisation and experience of software art in general. On this last point, the practice of live coding exemplifies how the practice of coding, its writing, working, and creative use, establishes an unstable relation to its output. In this sense, although of course code largely determines its output, the broader apparatus including the idiosyncrasies of the programmer provide indeterminate outcomes and help to stress the expressive dimension of software production as a whole.

Beginning with these ideas, the book establishes that program code, like language in general, evokes complex processes by which multiple voices can be expressed, modified, and further developed. With code, clearly problems can be solved in a multiplicity of ways, as evident on the Rosetta Code website, where as many different languages as possible are collected that relate to the same computational task,[23] or on Instructionset, a website where instructions are posted and programmers are invited to carry them out in a variety of ways.[24] Like other collective speech acts, programming oscillates between process and expression. This further resonates in the ways program code opens up broader discussions around the production of meaning and criticism, for it is clear that there are a myriad ways of saying hello in a multiplicity of human and machine languages, and a great complexity in the ways that the human-computer interprets them.[25] Take, for another example, the esoteric programming language Piet which looks like a geometric painting by Piet Mondrian, from which it takes its name.[26]

Like speech in relation to text, esoteric languages that diverge from the conventions of written language seem to stress the point that rendering speech or code as mere

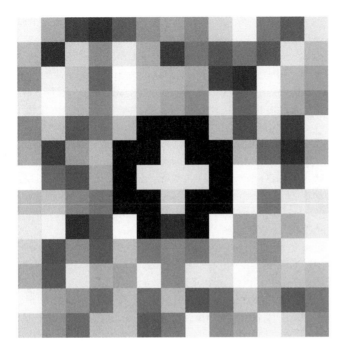

Figure 0.1
Source code written in the language Piet (original in color). Prints "*Hello, world!*" (http://
www.retas.de/thomas/computer/programs/useless/piet/explain.html). Image cc by-sa 2.5 license,
Thomas Schoch (2006).

written words fails to articulate the richness of human-machine expression. Similarly,
Kittler explains that there is something paradoxical about using words to write about
program code: "For one, all words from which the program was by necessity produced
and developed only lead to copious errors and bugs; for another, the program will
suddenly run properly when the programmer's head is emptied of words."[27] The
paradox opens up some interesting opportunities for coding practices that challenge
expectations of what source code does in itself and what it might do once run. In this
way the use of esoteric languages like Befunge, Brainfuck, or Piet somewhat undermine
the interpellative authority of the computer and stress alternative interpretations like
the paradoxical qualities of speech. Perhaps we can begin to think of these examples
as excitable program code.

Coding expression

Some core principles underpin the practices of coding as both procedure and expression. Of course, computers don't really speak but follow prescribed rules of execution,

tasks, and actions. Nevertheless, there is more to coding than simply the demonstration of formal logic, as if everything could be reduced to binary representation at a fundamental level. The conventions of writing and reading, of both text and code, might be considered to be part of coded systems of input and output (abbreviated as I/0), and yet formal logic fails to break the apparent paradox of language. In *The Art of Computer Programming* (1968), Donald Knuth already emphasized the depth of the relationship between writing a computer program and the logic that underpins it— what he referred to as "literate programming"—and so acknowledged programming to be somewhat like composing poetry or music.[28] He also demonstrated how reading could be understood as procedural and reflexive in his "Procedures for Reading This Set of Books." A short extract: "5. Is the subject of the chapter interesting you? If so, go to step 7; if not, go to step 6. . . . 14. Are you tired? If not, go back to step 7; 15. Go to sleep. Then, wake up, and go back to step 7."[29]

The physical form of a text and book, such as the one you are reading (if it still interests you), contributes to the production of meaning in the way that contextual information does in general. The text simply cannot be divorced from the materials and institutions that produce and disseminate it. In *Writing Machines*, N. Katherine Hayles puts it this way: "When a literary work interrogates the inscription technology that produces it, it mobilizes reflexive loops between its imaginative world and the material apparatus embodying that creation as a physical presence."[30] Like M. C. Escher's lithograph *Drawing Hands* (1948), in which two hands draw each another on a sheet of paper, there are many examples of recursion that encourage the author or reader to reflect on their role within the construction of the text, and on the ways in which meaning is constructed. Discussions of this tend to emphasize the link to literary theory (famously explored in Barthes's essay "The Death of the Author")[31] but also to second-order cybernetics, in terms of the way the observer is understood to produce changes to the system being observed,[32] akin to what Gregory Bateson referred to as "recursive epistemology."[33] Informed by systems thinking, Bateson understood recursion to operate on all levels across natural and cultural forms, undermining hierarchical orders of knowledge.

Another useful concept from Bateson, "double description," reinforces the importance of bringing together two or more information sources in order to provide information that is different from either one of them.[34] In a similar way, the combination of formal description and creative action, what might be referred to as *double coding*, is well established in software arts practice and where program code is made "literate." What has become known more specifically as "codework" provides a good example of how the practices of writing and programming can recombine formal logic and poetic expression. Sometimes referred to as pseudo-code, and often nonexecutable, codeworks operate in a similar realm to esoteric programs, and confound any easy assumptions about how meanings are produced prescriptively. Such examples also serve to undermine the idea that execution is the sole site of interpretation for code.

A double sense of interpretation lies at the core of this, and suggests a broader engagement with critical literacy (literary criticism for computing) that includes code and other written or spoken forms. Indicative of this tendency is Mez's hybrid language "mezangelle" (developed in the 1990s) which simultaneously combines formal structures from code and speech into a kind of creole, thus challenging some of the assumptions of what constitutes communicative exchange between humans and machines, meshing together speaking-working-coding into new forms that reflect contemporary communication systems. Her intention is to expand the ways that meanings are generated beyond the conventions of written language, as explained using mezangelle:

```
2 4m a text fromme the ground[ing] uppe
2 n-hance the simple text of an email thru the splicing of wurds
2 phone.tic[k-tock]aulli m-bellish a tract ov text in2 a neo.logistic
maze
2 network 2 the hilt N create de[e]pen.den[ting]cies on email lizts for
the wurkz dis.purse.all
2 graphi.caulli N text.u.alli e-voke a conscious sens.u.all & lingual mix
2 make net.wurkz space themz.elves in2 a spindle of liztz thru
collaboratori n-tent
2 uze computer kode kon.[e]vent.ionz spliced with irc emoticons and
ab[scess]breviations
2 spout punctu[rez]ationz reappropri.[s]ated in2 sentence schematics
2 polysemicalli m-ploy a fractured wurdset
2 m-brace 4m conventionz
2 flaunt pol[emic]itical l-usions
2 ig.gnaw word endinz
2 let lettahs b used as subsetz
2 x-tend N promote n-clusive meaningz.[35]
```

The example, using a technique referred to as double (or multiple) coding, exemplifies the material aspects of code both on a functional and an expressive level, even if it further confuses interpretation by its nonfunctionality or inability to communicate clearly (which is part of the point, of course). In this sense, nonexecutable (or illiterate) code can also be considered to be a command that fails to interpellate the reader, and thus promotes the notion that all commands are open to failure and errors, just as refusing to act is a provocation in other contexts. So too with obfuscated code contests, where it is clear that program code has an aesthetic dimension that extends beyond the conventions of programming which stress the efficiency and brevity of source code. In taking to an extreme the principle that program code be concise, a program might also be seen to run in rather unpredictable and amusing ways that confound the expectations of the human and machine reader-interpreter and allow them to rethink their prejudices.[36]

The double description evident in programming, and arguably inherent to it, can open up ambiguities and imaginative feedback loops. Indeed the loop is an important component of imperative programming, indicating when instructions are to be repeated or set to repeat until a terminating condition is met, unless an infinite loop is invoked. Programs are often structured around an infinite loop, known as the event loop; but with the use of infinite loops comes the possibility of infinite growth, which threatens the logical structure of the machine. Strategies like "deprogramming" bring to attention the structures and standardized formats of programs in this way. In the following example, from the website deprogramming.us,[37] a hello world program written in Perl has been modified to repeat itself in an endless loop:

```
#!/usr/bin/perl
# prozac.pl
# it will greet your system to death.
# but you go down in a cheerful endless loop.

while (1) {
        print "Hello World!\n";
        system ("$0"); # this line replicates it.
}
```

A simple example like this reflects the disruptive capacity of critical aesthetics to comment on the operations and effects of computational processes more broadly, working, as Alan Kay has referred to it, at the level of the "metamedium" (both performing universal computation and simulating all other media).[38]

Moreover, there is a danger of overstating the role of code as the source of action unless it is considered as part of a wider set of communicative actions by multiple human and nonhuman agents. Indeed, if code speaks, under what conditions and on behalf of whom?[39] Referring to code as speechlike becomes significant for this reason, as it invokes an established tradition considering speech to be more intelligible than writing, and its importance for critical debate and understanding of action in the world. To Socrates, who allegedly did not write his philosophy but spoke it, the voice is the "unwritten law" pertaining to the moral law, in contrast to the written law. It takes on a kind of authority and authenticity in this way and carries the inner voice of moral integrity.[40] One should not overstate the role of speech either, and clearly it contains its own internal contradictions and inherent paradoxes. Yet the spoken word does appear to haunt all texts as "sound is the natural habitat of language," as Walter J. Ong puts it in *Orality and Literacy*, and even writing needs to speak (if only silently) to reveal its meanings to the reader-listener.[41] Ong also makes a similar point to Kittler, pointing to the paradox that in expressing ideas about orality, he relies on the written form rather than a spoken performance to deliver the argument. Part of the difficulty in writing something down is that the transformative possibilities of speech are curtailed.

Like executable code, there is something *overdetermined* about all writing in this sense. In "Talking Back," bell hooks stresses the inherent politics of forms of writing that hold on to speech, for both writing and speech can express resistance to forms of power—as with the rejection of capital letters in her name.[42] Is this what some programs do, too, in holding on to the special qualities and paradoxes of speech? More than simply writing, program code is a special kind of writing and, unlike a score that is followed but interpreted, it follows its script quite literally. It holds on to its script and does not let go, but in so doing it also and importantly holds on to the inherent special qualities and paradoxes of speech, its predeterminations and its sense of excess.[43]

Introduction

The purpose of the book is to explore these double descriptions: involving both formal logic and the expressive aspects of coding, its constraints and its excesses. To some readers, it may seem rather unfashionable to concentrate on spoken language as the main referent: why not use mathematics as the main metaphor for analysis, given that the computer works through binary arithmetic—both representing and manipulating numbers in a system of 0s and 1s? Such an approach might also be expressed in the interest in "object-oriented ontology" and its allusion to object-oriented programming, with a return of attention to the discrete object rather than relations,[44] as well as in numerical articulations of politics. In *Number and Numbers*, Alain Badiou writes: "We live in the era of number's despotism. . . . Number governs our conception of the political."[45] Indeed the relation between the human and machine reader comes closer than ever to the operations of a machine performing calculations. However, the book attempts to address this problem the other way around, insisting on a discourse that derives from an understanding of the human condition and of politics that operates through language rather than simply through the economy. Moreover, the problem identified here is the invasion of language by economics. The universal calculating machine has sharpened our understanding of the operations of speech and writing, not least through what Ong calls "secondary orality," through writing technologies that produce scores and scripts.[46] But under the present conditions of financial capitalism, human action is rendered economic and its force is annulled, as it is "expressed not with words but with numbers," as Boris Groys put it.[47] To Groys, the task is to transcribe the world from the medium of money to that of language, so that politics can operate freely in relation to fate rather than being subordinate to the economy. Speech continues to underscore the human condition, however paradoxical this may appear.

These are some of the initial ideas that account for the book's attention to speech, its relation to the human condition, and its continued importance within cultural criticism. The book is not intended to be philosophy or theory as such. It takes critical writing to be a form of practice, and the many examples of code add to this conviction, not as illustrations but as additional forms of criticism. The resurgent interest in the concept of speech and the voice in recent years has something to do with the perceived neglect of sound in cultural work, no doubt,[48] but for the purpose of the book it is also an opportunity to foreground speech and action in the spirit of Hannah Arendt's writings,[49] and to consider some recent work that identifies how both speech and action appear to have lost their power, not least to mathematical symbols. To put it simply, *speech continues to need a voice that exceeds number.*

These are some starting points for the book and an indication of the broad sweep and eclecticism of its references. The first chapter, "Vocable Code" (co-written with Alex McLean), examines the performative and expressive dimension of programming and provides a number of examples. The aim is to stress some of the instabilities of code that undermine strict determinations of intention and meaning. Accordingly, the chapter looks in more detail at the linguistic analogies between code and natural languages, and the ways these have been understood in terms of meaning production. Speech emanates from the human body; computer programs have bodies too, and various attempts at simulation have revealed the impossibility of duplication. The further link of speaking to thinking machines demonstrates the sophistication of the human apparatus and the enduring complexity of speech, both as a sign of intelligence and as one that requires social interactions. Indeed collective speech acts provide multiple ways of understanding the complexities of code and the performative actions of running code. This is where speech indicates a more open-ended set of procedures that do not entirely compute, and that operate both within and beyond computational processes.

The second chapter, "Code Working," emphasizes a more overt political dimension of working with code, by stressing the ways in which all codework necessarily carries with it the work that has been invested in its production, as well as in the broader apparatuses through which it is served. This partly explains the motivation for many software producers to reveal the source code as an integral part of their work, particularly in the production of codeworks previously mentioned. A number of other examples are introduced, especially work by artists and programmers keen to offer alternatives to mainstream development, ranging from the performances of the live-coding scene to commons-based peer production. These demonstrate that new ideas emerge through wider recursive processes, which reflect the communicative and linguistic dimensions of work and action. If the first chapter established that code was speechlike, then this chapter further establishes that speech has become more codelike under the conditions of informational capitalism, especially when work is executed through scores and scripts, something that Paolo Virno argues in building upon Arendt's work.[50] Taking Virno's line of argument, the relationship of capital to language also helps to establish how working can be understood as speech acts, facilitated by networked communications technologies and collective formations of work. This underpins the ways in which commodified technologies have appropriated collective speech acts and networked intelligence. It also allows for the possibility of code operating in excess of market forces and, despite the title of the chapter, more in the realm of code action than code work.

The third chapter, "Coding Publics," builds on many of the same references but focuses more on collective action and reconceptualizing ideas of publicness, again making reference to the writings of Arendt. The voice undermines this public dimension by offering a dual representational function, indicating both the precondition for language acquisition and also the expression of political opinion. That the idea of democracy itself is in crisis, along with the voice, is revealed in a range of paradoxes over the terms in use, and also over key issues that relate to intellectual property and the uneasy interconnections between free software and free speech. For Christopher M. Kelty, again referring to Arendt, the free software movement is an example of emergent and self-organizing public actions, underpinned by the sharing of source code.[51] With the free software movement in mind, he introduces the term "recursive public" to account for the ways in which the public is able to reconstitute itself as a public, through the modification of the platform through which it speaks and by addressing other technical and legal layers of operation. This attention to publicness has implications also for the connection to property regimes and the ways that social technologies (especially popular platforms like Twitter and Facebook) tend to encourage ever more voices to be heard but only with restricted registers and effects. The concern is to consider some of the mainstream implementations of social software, to register the conditions under which this is done and the language employed to do so, and to examine the consequences in terms of the production of social relations and subjectivities. Through their reliance on proprietary logic, these developments seem to legislate against a plurality of voices that have unique attributes, which Arendt considers to be necessary for politics. Although there may be more voices speaking, they are effectively made mute. Against popular interpretations of them, the logic of networks and the rhetorical promises of social media are examined as effective mechanisms for the *suppression* of political expression in the public realm, and to reveal how public intellect is becoming ever more privatized through free-market logic. The coalition between consumer capitalism and democracy is evident in relation to certain platforms that claim to allow enhanced participation in the political process, where again the voice is strongly invoked but only in compromised forms. It would seem that social media not only fail to provide the means for people to have an effective voice but also reinforce neoliberal values, paradoxically through technologies that appear to promote the voice across telecommunications networks and online sharing platforms. This leads to the final section of the third chapter, in which the concept of the speaking public is reimagined not simply in its ability to enter into discourse but in its ability to modify the very platform through which it operates. And yet this capacity to express opinions is bound both to collective action and to the forces of domination, in reciprocal relation. Thus participation and collective forms of political expression become part of the very mechanism of guaranteeing their nullification. Clearly something important is missing.

The final chapter, "Code for-Itself," moves toward a summary of key issues, drawing on Franco Berardi's *The Soul at Work* (already introduced in the earlier chapter on work) to illustrate how the voice relates to material factors emanating from the way capital tries to incorporate both the soul and voice into production.[52] If the soul was once considered the source of speech, now conditions of contemporary production appear to have colonized both, indicating the politics of work to involve a broader set of issues that include speech acts and the communications platforms through which we speak. Voice reenters the discussion, on account of the need to focus on the biopolitical preconditions and the most fundamental aspect of human expression. In this way, the voice stands for the sensitivity of a culture bound by calculation and by neoliberalism's emptying out of expressive language. The ability to voice things is offered, if not accelerated, but is ultimately rendered illusionary by political forces that do not care about the "grain of the voice,"[53] as it lies outside the interests of the market and profiteering.

One of the main problems identified is the way the acquisition of language and the human condition have been largely separated as part of the expansion of market logic. More than simply a series of sounds from the body, a speech act is something that involves the human capacity to think and thereby express feelings. Rediscovering the voice, combined with words as speech, is therefore a necessary part of social transformation in the face of overpowering forces that close down and oversimplify discussion, or reduce action to procedures and behaviors that can be simulated. If human action is compromised by its contemporary expression in numbers, it should also be remembered that even at binary level, in terms of numerical calculations, the computer is surprisingly prone to errors, and certain calculations simply cannot be performed by strings of binary digits (determining the value of pi is a famous example).[54] Further ambiguities arise in computational processes when complex formations are introduced such as "or," "and," "not," as well as the infinite loops already mentioned. Once code is likened to speech, it also provides the possibility of new forms of criticism and practice that combine natural and artificial languages into new speech acts, in which ideas are stated and then reflected upon and restated. For all languages are a mode of action in this way, and not only a referent of thinking. If coding is an invitation for speech and action—a script to be executed—then the act of coding is a deliberate action across cultural and technological fields. In this way it offers the potential to open up some of the inherent paradoxes of double description. This is a similar point to Groys's assertion that politics needs to operate with language if it is to act freely, and that the critical task is to assert its internal paradox. Under present conditions of capitalism, human action functions as a commodity, that is to say, it is inherently mute.[55]

The example that ends this chapter is a script that attempts to connect to a web server on each of the 4,294,967,296 IPv4 Internet addresses in turn. Where successful, it posts the message "Hello world!" to the server. The script signals other possibilities for speech, both *within* and *beyond* politics.[56] Perhaps programmers need to find their voices in this respect, such that their scripts might begin to announce themselves to the world in ways that remain open to other expressive possibilities and collective actions. By acting collectively, in the echoes of others in the act of speech (as Butler puts it), some of the rules of correct speech can be broken, and meaning can be reconnected to the body.[57] Similarly, babbling, or different forms of nonstandard speech, can extend the political and aesthetic possibilities of speech. This is how the following chapter begins, with reference to sound poetry that disrupts linguistic rules and rejects the authority of the master's voice.[58] Speech is inherently political in this sense, and programs characterized in this way provide ever more possibilities for generating unpredictable results in recognition of a body politic.

```
#!/usr/bin/python
# A script for greeting every server on the Internet.
import iptools, httplib
for ip in iptools.IpRangeList('0.0.0.0/0'):
  try:
    print "Greeting " + ip
    cx = httplib.HTTPConnection("%s:80" % ip)
    cx.request("POST", '/', "message=Hello+world!")
  except:
    pass
```

1 Vocable Code

If program code is like speech inasmuch as it does what it says, then it can also be said to be like poetry inasmuch as it involves both written and spoken forms.[1] The analogy to poetry suggests numerous aesthetic and critical possibilities for code, beyond its serving simply as functional instructions.[2] There are many examples of programmers working in this spirit, referring to the "poiesis" of code (its making), and working with the connections between the structural and syntactic qualities of written code and poetry, or in spoken performances where source code is read aloud as if a poem; Franco Berardi reading the source code of the "I Love You" virus in 2001 is one such example.[3] This esoteric practice makes historical reference to artists expressing language as found material and arbitrary noise, in bruitist poetry and simultaneous poems from the Dada period for example, where texts in different languages were read aloud at the same time. Using these ideas as a point of departure, this chapter aims to draw attention to the aesthetic aspects of programs but particularly to their speech-like qualities, to make apparent the vocable elements that underpin some of the unstable aspects of coding practices.

Pertinent to the initial discussion are the Dadaist "sound poems" of Kurt Schwitters, who described his method of combining diverse elements to undermine the boundaries between aesthetic forms. A deliberate confusion was produced, somewhat similar to coding practices in which written form and output are conflated. In the case of Schwitters, output was expressed through his arrangements of what he called the "banalities" of objects and language by focusing on vocables (the recognizable elements that are capable of being spoken). Treating these like data open for reassemblage, he explains: "These materials are not to be used logically in their objective relationships, but only within the logic of the work of art. The more intensively the work of art destroys rational objective logic, the greater the possibilities of artistic form. Just as in poetry word is played off against word, so in this instance one will play off factor against factor, material against material."[4]

This explains how his language experiments play with unorthodox combinations and lack of referentiality. For example, *Ursonate* (1922–1932) is a sound poem composed of nonlexical vocables (strings of phonemes that make "non-words") performed by Schwitters himself entirely from memory. The full poem is highly structured, arranged in four movements over a total of 29 pages, and takes approximately 30 minutes to read. An excerpt follows (and you can hear a recorded recital at UbuWeb):

```
Fümms bö wö tää zää Uu,
                    pögiff,
                        kwii Ee.

Oooooooooooooooooooooooooo,
    dll rrrrr beeeee bö
    dll rrrrr beeeee bö fümms bö,
        rrrrr beeeee bö fümms bö wö,
            beeeee bö fümms bö wö tää,
                bö fümms bö wö tää zää,
                    fümms bö wö tää zää Uu:⁵
```

The phonetic aspects of the human voice are foregrounded at the expense of more conventional understandings through semantics and syntax, and in this way the poem is more directly grounded in the sound-making apparatus of the body (close to what some call "pure meaning," a single, simple sound or tone, free from mixture or combination). Yet even in their abstraction, the sounds would be familiar to any German speaker (like Schwitters himself), who would understand them relative to precise learned movements of their own vocal tract. In one sense, this is poetry about the shape of words in the mouth, and the direct, perhaps synesthetic relationship between mouth shape and the sound generated.

The last part of this excerpt from the *Ursonate* features a progressive scan across part of the vocabulary of the piece, each line taking in a new word at the end and removing one from the beginning, giving a sense of movement across a symbolic textual structure. The listing below in the Haskell programming language attempts to represent this structure, and can be considered "successful" in that when this code is interpreted, the original text is produced. It includes the list of words and an algorithm for progressively scanning across the list. The subtleties of the original—a short first line and a concluding colon—take up the majority of the code, and the result is not much shorter than the original. It is different, however, in that it makes structure explicit that is only implicit in the score, describing more than the surface text. In this respect the code is perhaps closer to the poem as it was spoken than to the poem as written, with the intonation of the reader relating structural information that can only be inferred from the written text. The code is a kind of paralinguistic phrasing, and on interpretation produces its own transcription with this phrasing removed. It oscillates between written and spoken forms.

```
poem = recite sounds
sounds = words "dll rrrrr beeeee bö fümms bö wö tää zää Uu"

recite xs | xs == sounds = (unwords $ take 4 xs) ++ "\n" ++ recite (tail xs)
          | length xs == 6 = slice xs ++ ":\n"
          | otherwise = slice xs ++ ",\n" ++ recite (tail xs)
    where slice xs = (unwords $ take 6 xs)
```

Evidently sound poetry may be nonlexical but is not entirely ambiguous. Schwitters makes this clear in an accompanying text that declares the poem should be performed using German intonation, emphasizing our earlier comments about the shape of the words in the mouth. For without a method of interpreting the text into sound, whether explicit or implied, this could not be considered a sound poem as such. The method of interpretation is external to the text, but at the same time a fundamental part of the experience of the work. The same relationship of code and interpreter is apparent with computer code; a running program exists as a combination of the code with a language interpreter. Indeed it is possible to write one piece of source code that conforms to the grammatical rules of several quite different programming languages, and that behaves differently in each. It is also possible to write source code that when interpreted outputs source code in different languages—and this is a standard process in the interpretation of C code. The example further demonstrates that a computer program can undermine the distinction between its function as a score and its performance, in similar ways to the sound poem (but in quite different ways to conventional musical scores).

This chapter aims to extend this discussion about the relation between spoken language and program code, but in particular to speculate on vocable code and the ways in which the body is implicated in coding practices. Through the connection to speech, programs can be called into action as utterances that have wider political resonance; they express themselves as if possessing a voice.

Coding language

To attempt to understand a "text" like a sound poem requires recognition that all languages consist of closed systems of discrete semiotic elements, and that meaning is organized out of differences between elements that are meaningless in themselves.[6] Things can only be understood in terms of the organizational structure of which they are a part; there is an abstract system (langue/competence) that generates the concrete event (parole/performance) in semiotic terms.[7] The extreme of this position is the view that a text is entirely autonomous from the act of writing—writing writes, not writers— as if all writing is active like a computer program or has a kind of agency beyond its inscription.[8] It is as if every work carries its source code with it through the formal logic that underpins its behavior, whether emanating from a computer or from a book or speech.[9] In this respect it speaks for itself.

Grammars

To understand in more detail more how a script performs, one common starting point is the linguistic concept of transformational grammar, derived from Noam Chomsky's *Syntactic Structures* of 1957. Chomsky assumes that somehow grammar is given in advance, hard-wired or preprogrammed: that humans possess innate grammatical competence that is presocial (and one of the controversies of Chomsky's system is its separation of consciousness from the outside social world). Thus he explains the deep-seated rules by which language operates and how principles and processes are set by which sentences are generated. In procedural terms, a natural language can be simply described as a "finite state Markov process that produces sentences from left to right."[10] In mathematics and other formalized systems, the logic adheres to similar grammars that generate their own grammatical sequences. Chomsky's conclusion is that grammar is independent of meaning, and that the separation from semantics is essential to the study of syntactic structure.

Clearly syntax is also fundamental for the structure of a statement in a computer language, such as with the use of parentheses to produce subclauses while retaining the overall flow of logic. Conditional structures such as loops are commonplace in setting out instructions to perform repeated tasks, usually stopped under a certain condition, and loops rest within loops in intricate ways, including parenthesis within parenthesis (as with the appearance of { and }). With loops, simple sentences are able to reproduce themselves recursively, as in the example by Douglas Hofstadter: "The sentence I am now writing is the sentence you are now reading."[11] The referent "the sentence" is understandable only within the overall context of the words that make a sentence, this being one of the key structural elements of written language as a whole. Evidently it would be a mistake to think that grammars are simply devices for generating sentences, and much experimental software artwork has been developed with this principle in mind, partly in response to the overreliance on the syntactical aspects of coding and to address issues of meaning production at source.[12] Whereas artists simply had to engage with programming in early computer arts or generative arts practice, the lack of this necessity now (due to the wide availability of scripting languages with libraries of functions) allows for wider issues to be engaged related to semantic and social concerns.

This view also recognizes the wider material apparatus of programming and the many agents of production involved in the process, which would include the engineers who design the machines and the workers who build them as well as the programmers who write the programs.[13] Meanings are produced through the interactions of these agents at all levels of operation. In "There Is No Software," Kittler argues that software obscures such operations, and as a result confusion arises between the use of formal and everyday languages. Programming languages have supplemented natural languages, suggesting the need for new literacies that include both natural and artificial languages.[14] These languages form a "postmodern tower of Babel," as he puts it, and this is why: "We simply do not know what our writing does."[15] Kittler is partly referring to the ways that graphical interfaces dispense with the need for writing and hide the "machine" from its users. The confusion Kittler refers to is implemented at the level of hardware itself, wherein "so-called protection software has been implemented in order to prevent 'untrusted programs' or 'untrusted users' from any access to the operating system's kernel and input/output channels."[16] If that was at issue in the early 1990s when these words were written, the problem of access to the code that underpins the system hardware is now exaggerated with contemporary developments in service-based computing; now users hardly know at all what their programs do nor have access to them, as they are closed off almost entirely from their machines.

Behind this crucial issue of access to information is the history of the sharing of source code, itself rooted in the history of the UNIX operating system and its precarious position between the promises of the public domain and commercial enterprise, corresponding to the differences between free software and open-source development.[17] The former champions the idea of freedom in resistance to proprietary software by keeping software in the public domain (associated with Richard Stallman and the free software movement), while the latter takes the view that open-source development will lead to better implementation and therefore offers economic benefit (associated with Eric Raymond and his free-market approach). According to Raymond, UNIX is open as it works across different computer platforms, and as such it is the "closest thing to a hardware-independent standard for writing truly portable software."[18] In supporting multiple program interfaces and flexibility, it provides access to the hidden depths of the machine. Furthermore, it emanates from a "bottom-up" folk tradition in which expertise comes from the culture itself, exemplified in principles of transparency and discoverability, and indeed in the software engineering ethos to "keep it simple, stupid!"[19]

Also with UNIX in mind, but arguing against Kittler's determinism, Florian Cramer has drawn on terms from Roland Barthes's *S/Z* to make the distinction between "readerly" and "writerly" texts.[20] Rather than the readerly properties of a GUI operating system that hides the underlying program code, Cramer claims the command line user interface of UNIX is writerly, in terms of its openness and in encouraging the reader to become an active producer of "scriptable" code. For Cramer, these writerly aspects of coding break down the false distinction between the writing and the tool with which the writing is produced (and in terms of the computer, between code and data). He cites a 1998 essay by Thomas Scoville, "The Elements of Style: UNIX as Literature," to insist on the writerly aspects of programming by explaining how writers use language: "No literary writer can use language merely as a stopgap device with which to compose an artwork that is not in itself language—so, like in a recursive loop, literature writes its own instrumentation."[21] This is a kind of writing that writes itself; all writing is a kind of program in this sense.

Notation and execution are collapsed into one thing, as in the Fluxus performance score of La Monte Young's *Composition 1961 No. I, January I,* "Draw a straight line and follow it," that Cramer uses as an example of software art (interestingly, an example that does not use a computer).[22] Another example might be Alvin Lucier's composition *I am sitting in a room (for voice on tape)* (1969),[23] a script read by a performer and repeated 32 times as a loop. The score explains the concept like a program: at each iteration, the sound is recorded, played back, and then rerecorded, and hence becomes a representation of the resonance of the room itself as well as the body of the speaker. The instruction is executed, but the work is more about the irregularities of speech (including Lucier's stutter) and its inherent musicality, to reveal that speech is so much more than the articulation of words.[24] But also the words themselves can be said to perform, as they execute their instructions recursively.

The point is that neither the score nor the program script can be detached from its performance, and in this context this is what makes a program like speech. The following example renders the word "speak" as ASCII characters, which are reversed horizontally and vertically to create a symmetrical arrangement. However, the character forms somewhat mask the symmetry from the human eye, and the reader might need to turn to the code to verify the act of speech.

```
example@speakingcode:code$ cat <(paste <(echo
speak|figlet|tac|rev) <(echo speak|figlet|tac)) <(paste <(echo
speak|figlet|rev) <(echo speak|figlet))
 |_|                    |_|
\_\|_|_,__\|___\ /_. /___|    |___/ ._/ \___|\__,_|_|\_\
 <    | |_( /__  | )_| \ __\    \__ \ |_) |  _/ (_| |    <
 / /| | `_ /\ _ / \ _' |__ /    / __| '_ \ / _ \/ _` | | |/ /
 __ | |_ __ ___   __ _ ___      ___ _ __  ___  __ _| | __

      _                                 _
   __ | |_ __ ___   __ _ ___      ___ _ __  ___  __ _| | __
 / /| | `_ /\ _ / \ _' |__ /    / __| '_ \ / _ \/ _` | | |/ /
 <    | |_( /__  | )_| \ __\    \__ \ |_) |  _/ (_| |    <
\_\|_|_,__\|___\ /_. /___|    |___/ ._/ \___|\__,_|_|\_\
             |_|                  |_|
```

Notation

Rather than include writing systems such as program code, most critical work in this area has contrasted spoken and written forms of language. But much of the subjective expression of speech is hidden when it is transcribed in written form, and there are many simple techniques, which we tend to take for granted, that try to capture the special qualities of speech with various degrees of success. Approaches to quotation are particularly interesting in this connection, and what became the common practice of using the markup convention of quotation marks to distinguish the voice of the character in the text from that of the writer. Quotation or exclamation marks emphasize that the words are not simply printed but are spoken in written form. Similarly in coding practices, "commenting out" is used to distinguish the voice of the program from that of the programmer.

```
# This is the voice of the programmer
echo "This is the voice of the program"
```

Yet the program interpreter only listens to the program and not the programmer; and significant comments, existing as natural language read by programmers, are ignored by interpreters, as with the numerous instances of the word "fuck" that can be found in the comments of the Linux kernel. Here is one example:

```
alex@quantas:/tmp/linux-3.0-rc5$ find -name '*.c' |xargs grep -i fuck
./lib/vsprintf.c: * Wirzenius wrote this portably, Torvalds fucked it
up:-)
```

Comments are not the only aspects of programs ignored during interpretation, as the majority of the text may be discarded and optimized away in the early stages. Carefully chosen variable names are replaced with numbers, and explanatory two-dimensional spatial arrangements are compressed into contiguous, single-dimensional sequences. Nor is the color highlighting seen in programming interfaces saved to source files. Together these aspects of programs are known as "secondary notation," a pejorative term suggesting that code's primary purpose is to be executed by a computer, and only secondarily to be understood by a human. However, in terms of human understanding, the names given to abstractions, their spatial arrangement, and their appearance on the page are as important as the logic contained within. If secondary notation is removed from a program then confusion results; and with human aspects of code removed, all that remains are monotonous sequences of syntax, bereft of meaning at the level of programming or wider human understanding of the processes at work.

The interpreter ignores natural words, but they still remain in the original source code, giving the opportunity for programmers to express themselves beyond the internal actions of the computer. In his technical manual "Oracle PL/SQL: Guide to Oracle8i Features," Steven Feuerstein controversially placed technical examples in the context of war crimes.

```
CREATE OR REPLACE PROCEDURE update_tragedies (warcrim_ids
IN name_varray, num_victims IN number_varray) IS BEGIN
```

```
FOR indx IN warcrim_ids.FIRST .. warcrim_ids.LAST LOOP
UPDATE war_criminal SET victim_count = num_victims (indx)
WHERE war_criminal_id = warcrim_ids (indx); END LOOP; END;²⁵
```

This demonstrates the effectiveness of secondary notation, but as Oracle is used primarily in large-scale businesses, including much of the global financial infrastructure, Feuerstein's examples of excessive CEO compensation, union busting, and war crimes in a mainstream published book about technology were met with an outcry.[26] A similar approach to combining technical and political commentary can be seen in the following extract from Harwood's *Perl Routines to Manipulate London*, porting William Blake's poem "London" (of 1792) into the Perl programming language.[27] In both the original version and the adaptation, statistics and the modulation of populations are used for social comment:

```
local @SocialClasses = qw(
        RentBoy YoungGirl-Syphalitic-Inoculator
        CrackKid WarBeatenKid ForcedFeatalAbortion
        );
```

The interpreter will instead "perceive" an abstract, tokenized version, somewhat like:

```
t_local @v1 = [t1, t2, t3, t4, t5]
```

Much of the meaning of the program and how it might be understood is simply ignored by the computer. The program may extract the original text "RentBoy" from the pointer "t1," but the context of the container name "SocialClasses" will have been lost, and the program itself will have no notion of what the word "RentBoy" means.

In terms of the literate application of the programming language Perl (developed by Larry Wall in 1987), Harwood is extending an established aesthetic practice referred to as "Perl poetry," the practice of writing poems that can be compiled as Perl code, made possible by the semantic qualities of Perl. Wall was emphasizing the point that code has expressive qualities, and the need for programmers to "express both their emotional and technical natures simultaneously."[28] The technique is effective as it manages to combine both primary and secondary notation, both syntactical and semantic registers, and the tension between human and machine interpretation is made painfully evident (so much so that you might imagine yourself to hear the screams).

```
local %InfantsScreamInFear;
# WoeOfEveryMan is the main method for constructing the
# InfantScreamInFear structure:
# If we find that say that the hash %{RentBoy} is defined
# with values then we add this to the hash %{InfantScreamInFear}
```

```
sub WoeOfEveryMan
    foreach my $Class (@SocialClasses){
        warn "New class = $Class\n";
        $InfantsScreamInFear->{Class} = %{$Class} if {Class};
    }
}

# In every cry of every Man,
# In every Infants cry of fear,
# In every voice: in every ban,
# The mind-forg'd manacles I hear
```

The interplay of the body of the code, the programmer's comments, and the human-machine reader express how hardware and software, text and code, are "embodied." The body is of course registered in the content (in the codework itself), in the narrator's body (the comments and secondary notation), but also in the bodies of all those humans involved in the production process, including the reader's body. This embodiment issue is something that N. Katherine Hayles asserts in *Writing Machines*: "Literary texts, like us, have bodies, an actuality necessitating that other materialities and meanings are deeply interwoven into each other."[29] Imaginative and political possibilities emerge from this recognition.

Indeterminism

As in speech, it is clear that there is a dynamic relation between what exists and what is possible, between past and present states, between concealing and revealing possibilities corresponding to the layers within computation itself. Part of this relates to digitalization as opposed to the use of analog systems, in which elements are not continuous but discrete units or objects. Hayles clarifies this sense of structure: "The act of making discrete extends through multiple levels of scale, from the physical process of forming bit patterns up through a complex hierarchy in which programs are written to compile other programs."[30] The hierarchical aspect is important in understanding how code is organized in deliberate ways, and thus how it can also be understood and theorized. Hayles explains how human speech is analog, emanating from a continuous stream of breath that forms phonemes that are more discrete. Writing makes these units yet more discrete through inscription. Programmers oscillate between these modes at the level of the human-computer interface, translating between machine behavior and human perception,[31] with the human made somewhat computerized and the computer somewhat anthropomorphized. Compiling and interpreting, although similar, are also distinct across human and machine platforms. Therefore it would be a mistake to simply conflate natural language and human intelligence with program code. This is also an issue that Ong refers to when he argues that although some computer languages resemble human languages, they are unlike them as they do not emanate from the unconscious but directly out of consciousness.[32] Although this may or may not be strictly the case, the point is that both modes interact in ways we do not fully comprehend.

The human dimension is registered in a multiplicity of ways in communication systems, as for instance in conceptual metaphor theory,[33] in which meaning can be understood as largely structured through spatial relationships relative to the body, unbound by syntax. Speech grounds language in the voice, and orientational metaphor grounds semantics in the body. It follows that computer software cannot have access to systems of meaning without at least some kind of reference to bodily relationships. This embodiment issue has become crucially important for understanding the interactive experience of computation, extending the limits of HCI (human-computer interaction) traditions.[34] Similarly emergent fields such as "tangible computing" and "social computing" strive to account for the ways in which humans interact with physical objects that are increasingly "augmented" with computational processes and interactions with the environment.[35] Programmers bring bodily meaning to their work by applying models of human perception, and by trying to account for the ways that other social bodies are drawn into the process of meaning production.

In opposition to this tendency, Edsger Dijkstra understands the world of programs and of people as totally separate. He thinks that "whereas machines must be able to execute programs (without understanding them), people must be able to understand them (without executing them). These two activities are so utterly disconnected—the one can take place without the other."[36] Yet computers embedded in the fabric of the human environment, increasingly with actuators and reacting sensors, require the encoding of interactions that are meaningful to humans.[37] Even computers have some sense of their own conditions, as for instance in the way that a standard laptop can now detect when it is being dropped, or getting too hot. Perhaps the most radical physical action that a computer can carry out is simply turning itself off; not quite self-immolation, but all transitory data is lost. The following example *monitor.upstart* is a configuration file for Linux systems. When the computer starts up, it checks the temperature, and if this is higher than the long-term global average of 14 degrees Celsius, it shuts the computer down again. As the operation of the computer itself creates heat, and its feed of electricity is dependent on the production of greenhouse gases, it expresses interaction on a global scale.

```
start on startup
exec if [`perl -pe 's/\D+(\d+).*/\1/' \
        /proc/acpi/thermal_zone/*/temperature` -gt 14] \
    then shutdown now \
    fi
```

As software becomes ubiquitous it becomes ever more connected to external processes, and programs no longer encode pure logic but human social behavior too. Such approaches recognize that systems are embedded in larger language systems where meanings are produced through social practices. In other words, computer programs have bodies in the sense that other materialities and meanings are deeply interwoven, and these necessarily exist as part of wider social relations.

Coding speech

Clearly speech emanates from the body; but even more fundamentally voice has been understood as a precondition of consciousness itself. Johann Gottfried Herder, writing at the end of the eighteenth century, helped establish that voice and speech were distinct terms (even if in dubious ways that marginalized certain types of people outside of "normal" language).[38] To Herder, marking a distinction from other animals, speech happened when the voice took on the inflection of the human institution of language.[39] Thus, once the human voice "spoke," it was understood to signify higher human reason and a world of signification, as opposed to a mere voice that might simply comprise a collection of nonlexical vocables. Yet it would seem that computer speech simulation is rather too rational, further complicating the distinctions.

Machines

So what would it take for a machine to speak convincingly? The problem of how to account for the voice is a recurring theme, indicative of the energies that lie outside of rational systems of representation and the human fascination with simulations of the strange noises that lay at the root of language. In the eighteenth century, Wolfgang von Kempelen's speech machine was allegedly the first that allowed the simulation not only of some speech sounds but of whole words and short sentences. Initiated in 1769, it was further developed in response to a call from the Imperial Academy of Arts and Sciences in St. Petersburg in 1780 offering a prize to construct a machine that could reproduce vowel sounds and explain their properties.

In his 1791 book *Mechanismus der menschlichen Sprache nebst Beschreibung einer sprechenden Maschine* (The mechanism of the human speech with the description of a speaking machine), Kempelen describes "die Sprech-Maschine" (the speaking machine) in close detail so that others might be able to reconstruct and improve it (thus distributing his plans under the terms and conditions of what we would now consider to be open-source hardware).[40] The machine comprised bellows like lungs to pump air into the voice box simulating a windchest, while a reed controlled the release of air alongside movable parts corresponding to lips, palate, tongue, and nostrils. The mouth was modified by hand to produce speech in combination with a series of valves. The speech machine was presented in a format that invited the public to suggest some words to be repeated by the machine. At the end, the machine was explained in detail, demonstrating that the intention was not simply to provide a mystifying spectacle

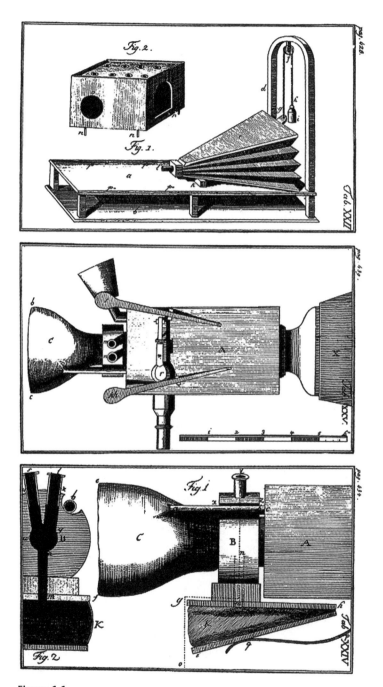

Figure 1.1
Wolfgang von Kempelen, "Sprech-Maschine" (1791), first developed in 1769. Image in public domain.

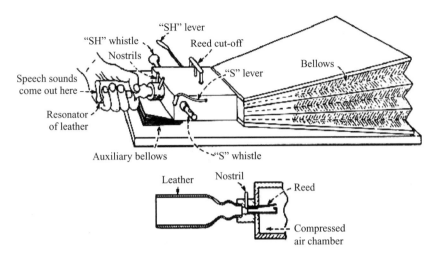

Figure 1.2
Reconstruction of Kempelen's talking machine, attributed to Sir Charles Wheatstone (1879). Image in public domain.

but to be of educational value, and more concretely, as Kempelen indicates, to give the deaf an instrument by which to produce speech. The idea was to simulate a voice in its fullest sense, following principles of free expression, to give voice to those without a voice, following in the spirit of what Kempelen refers to as "the basic tenets of society."[41] Significantly the machine did not simply reproduce the human speech organs but also attempted sound synthesis.[42]

There are far too many other historical attempts to capture speech to mention; but for the purpose of the argument being developed, it is worth stressing the enduring fascination of a machine that could capture human qualities and the many attempts to move beyond the limitations of the Latin alphabet. Phonography, developed in the early nineteenth century, was one such technique, in which each language sound was given a shorthand mark, Isaac Pitman even claiming (in 1854) his phonetic shorthand to be an exact "picture of speech" itself. Others who concentrated on the physiology of speech, such as Alexander Melville Bell (in 1849), described the "actual movements of the organs of speech"; Bell subsequently referred to his work as "visible speech," based on a universal notation system able to reproduce every dialect and language, the symbols of which were not alphabetical but physiological.[43]

These examples are among the myriad ways in which inventors of machines have tried to represent the complexities of what is spoken. This is also something that written languages have attempted using symbols; the Chinese language makes a notable example with its vast number of characters (the K'anghsi dictionary of Chinese in AD 1716 contained 40,545 characters and took about twenty years to learn, something that a computer might do more efficiently).[44] Another relevant example is Hangul, the main alphabet in use in what are now North and South Korea. Hangul was invented in the fifteenth century; not only is it phonetic, but the shapes of the consonants are based on the shape the mouth makes when the corresponding sound is made.[45] This grounding of symbols in the body also reinforces the idea that language might be recursive, undermining the distinction between the spoken word and the way it is produced (in a similar way to literature writing its own instrumentation, as previously mentioned).

These few examples also serve to emphasize the inadequacies of the Latin alphabet to capture dialects and phonetic diversity: making "the art of recording speech almost impossible" according to George Bernard Shaw, a position that he exemplifies in his play *Pygmalion*.[46] In the narrative, the main character Eliza Doolittle, the cockney flower girl, is the subject of a bet by a professor of phonetics that he can teach her gentility through the acquisition of proper speech. The title makes reference to the Greek myth in which Pygmalion, a sculptor, falls in love with a statue he carves, and Venus grants it the breath of life.[47]

The Pygmalion myth stands as a useful analogy for the idea of breathing life into machines. The chatterbot Eliza produced by Joseph Weizenbaum between 1964 to 1966, named after Eliza Doolittle, is a disarmingly simple example based on similar motivations: to simulate a believable exchange with a human conversant. It uses primitive natural-language processing to simulate a conversation with a therapist, producing human-like responses by implementing a simple script based on key words and language patterns through which responses are generated. Here is an example:

```
I am the psychotherapist. Please, describe your problems.
> Hello world.
Why do you say hello world?
> It's the orthodox way to begin when using a new computer language.
You have your mind on computers, it seems.
> Sometimes I think I am a computer.
You think too much about computers.
> Thinking computers, thinking too much about computers?
You should try taking your mind off of computers.
> Well you seem to dwell on the subject yourself too.
What makes you believe that?
> The evidence is in the above text!
Maybe your life has something to do with this.
```

Without involving complex algorithms, it can generate responses that appear to make some degree of sense. Yet it is interesting to note how the illusion of conversation follows an extremely reductive model of human expression, and the fantasies of machine intelligence seem to be similarly founded on reductive logic. At the same time, natural-language processing programs and other chatterbots offer good examples of the speechlike procedures mentioned thus far, as well as the apparent impossibility of duplicating actual speech.

Intelligence

To demonstrate believability, a machine would be required to possess some kind of intelligence that reflects the capacity for human reasoning, in parallel to turning mere voice sounds into proper speech that expresses human gentility. In a paper of 1950, "Computing Machinery and Intelligence," Alan Turing made the claim that computers would be capable of imitating human intelligence, or more precisely the human capacity for rational thinking. He set out what become commonly known as the "Turing test" to examine whether a machine is able to respond convincingly to an input with an output similar to a human's.[48] The contemporary equivalent, CAPTCHA (Completely Automated Public Turing test to tell Computers and Humans Apart), turns this idea around, so that the software has to decide whether it is dealing with a human or a script.[49] Perhaps it is the lack of speech that makes this software appear crude by comparison, as human intelligence continues to be associated with speech as a marker of reasoned semantic processing.

In his essay "Minds, Brains, and Programs" from 1980, John Searle refutes the Turing test because machines fall short in understanding the symbols they process. His observation is that the syntactical, abstract or formal content of a computer program is not the same as semantic or mental content associated with the human mind. The cognitive processes of the human mind can be simulated but not duplicated as such. Searle develops his thought experiment known as the "Chinese Room argument" as follows: "Suppose that I'm locked in a room and given a large batch of Chinese writing. Suppose furthermore (as is indeed the case) that I know no Chinese, either written or spoken. . . . To me, Chinese is just so many meaningless squiggles."[50] Given linguistic instruction, Searle imagines that he becomes able to answer questions that are indistinguishable from those of native Chinese speakers, but insists, "I produce the answers by manipulating uninterpreted formal symbols. As far as the Chinese is concerned, I simply behave like a computer; I perform computational operations on formally specified elements. For the purposes of the Chinese, I am simply an instantiation of the computer program."[51]

Searle's position is based on the linguistic distinction between syntax and semantics as applied to the digital computer or Turing machine as a "symbol-manipulating device," where the units have no meaning in themselves (a position that follows from semiotics). Even if it is argued that there is some sense of intentionality in the program or a degree of meaning in the unit, it is not the same as human information processing, and this sense of agency is what Searle calls "as-if intentionality." In the Chinese Room, Searle becomes an instantiation of a computer program, drawing on a database of symbols and arranging them according to program rules. The point to be stressed is that formal principles alone remain insufficient to demonstrate human reason; the Chinese language is a particularly complex kind of invention that challenges human capabilities (so that machines might usefully supplement them), but it also combines images and speech in ways that confound formal logic.

Also referring to the Chinese spoken by the "living reading machine," Ludwig Wittgenstein clarifies that a genuine speech act is more than just a series of sounds arranged in sequence, or talking without thinking. To him, "The sentence, as it were, plays a melody (the thought) on the instrument of the soul."[52] If the machine is considered to lack a soul, it is because it manipulates symbols but does not understand them or produce meanings in them. Wittgenstein likens this to the workings of a pianola, translating marks and following patterns rather than expressing intentionality as such: "The living reading machine produces as output solutions to arithmetical problems, texts spoken aloud, proofs of logical theorems, notes played on a piano, and suchlike. These 'machines' may be born, like an idiot savant, or trained."[53]

Although there are similarities with Searle's position and his description of "as-if intentionality," Wittgenstein's argument is different in that when a word is spoken it refers to "the whole environment of the event of saying it. And this also applies to our saying that someone speaks like an automaton or parrot."[54] The meanings of words are not derived from an inherent logical structure alone that manipulates symbols into particular sequences (like a program), but also from their social usage. This reveals a problem with the Searle experiment in that it is based on a description of the workings of the CPU (central processing unit) and not of the larger environment that has been stressed in earlier sections of this chapter, including the body and social relations.

Yet to Searle, the argument is posed rather differently. To him, in this specific case, the distinction between humans and machines is obsolete, as humans are already biological machines. It is possible for an artificial machine to think in principle, but only in simulation; for it to duplicate actual thought, it would also need to reproduce consciousness itself.[55] This may have proved impossible thus far, but the problem for Searle lies in the fact that computational processes do not simulate machines far enough in terms of energy.[56]

Embodiment

What is required to duplicate the human speech act more convincingly is a conscious body, and a model of human perception that is socially grounded sufficiently to be able to derive meaning and thus stake a claim of intelligence. For now, the position remains that machines still do not simulate human intelligence particularly convincingly, but it is also clear how willing humans are to anthropomorphize machines, especially those that appear to demonstrate the ability of speech. Speech seems to encapsulate, indeed embody, the complexities of meaning production, and therefore it comes as no surprise that there are repeated attempts and failures to simulate its procedures and melodies.

The various attempts to synthesize speech using computer systems seem to stress the point, although most attempts have involved taking recordings of small samples of real speech and concatenating them together. The sounds sampled are those made not when the vocal tract is held in a particular position (phonemes), but when the tract moves between two positions (diphones). An alternative to this, and closer to the principles of the speaking machine, is articulatory speech synthesis, in which a simulation is run of the lungs pushing air through the vocal cords, their oscillations producing air pressure waves shaped by the tongue, nose, teeth, and lips, each contributing their own smacks, grunts, whistles, and so on. For instance, Praat software, a speech analysis tool that can help visualize spoken language, attempts to simulate speech patterns.[57] In order for the synthesizer to say something, the articulatory synthesis package explains a number of necessary steps in biotechnical terms:

We are going to have the synthesizer say [əpə]. We need a Speaker and an Artword object.

1. Create a speaker with Create Speaker . . . from the New menu.
2. Create an articulation word of 0.5 seconds with Create Artword. . . .
3. Edit the Artword by selecting it and clicking View & Edit.
4. To set the glottis to a position suitable for phonation, use the ArtwordEditor to set the *Interarytenoid* activity to 0.5 throughout the utterance. You set two targets: 0.5 at a time of 0 seconds, and 0.5 at a time of 0.5 seconds.
5. To prevent air escaping from the nose, close the nasopharyngeal port by setting the *LevatorPalatini* activity to 1.0 throughout the utterance.
6. To generate the lung pressure needed for phonation, you set the *Lungs* activity at 0 seconds to 0.2, and at 0.1 seconds to 0.
7. To force a jaw movement that closes the lips, set the *Masseter* activity at 0.25 seconds to 0.7, and the *OrbicularisOris* activity at 0.25 seconds to 0.2.
8. Select the Speaker and the Artword and click Movie; you will see a closing-and-opening gesture of the mouth.
9. Select the Speaker and the Artword and click To Sound . . . (see Artword & Speaker: To Sound . . .).
10. Just click OK; the synthesis starts.

This example may express something of the energy that Searle identified as missing in previous simulations, but despite some promising results the vocal tract has so far proved too complex to fully understand in order to produce plausible speech, certainly in real time. Even the introduction to the Praat software admits its limitations: "Praat is a powerful tool from which you can learn a lot on your own, but if you want to improve your spoken English, we recommend you work with a qualified ESL instructor."

Artificial voices largely remain based on concatenative synthesis, in which emotional aspects are impossible to fully control and simulate. Articulatory synthesis stress, for instance, might be simulated as physical tightness, whereas with concatenative synthesis an actor's voice would have to be recorded making every combination of possible sounds while pretending to be stressed. This thinking can be seen in the everyday speech synthesis software that is now regularly bundled with operating systems, later combined with a range of sample voices and most recently with authentic-sounding breaths between sentences.[58] Nevertheless the concern here is not with speech synthesis per se, but rather with the impulse for the various attempts to simulate speech, which have largely failed despite massive increases in computational speed. The human nervous system and brain remain a massively concurrent system, and modern software struggles to run more than one interacting process at a time. In plain speech it is possible to pronounce two things at the same time, and this is something that the experiments of Schwitters would affirm. The enduring problem of how to invent a machine that can replicate the complexities of the human mouth and vocal cords attests to the power of speech but also to the continued difficulties of its duplication.

Code act

In charting the interactions of speech, writing, and the actions of code (and borrowing from Grusin and Bolter's idea of "remediation"), Hayles explains how new practices borrow and reinterpret previous technologies recursively.[59] Speech and writing both influence program code and are changed by program code. Taking inspiration, or rather a point of departure, from Ferdinand de Saussure (on speech) and Jacques Derrida (on writing), Hayles aims to examine the conceptual system in which code is embedded and the activity of coding. The significant fact for Hayles is not whether speech is subordinate to writing (the position that Derrida takes) or whether writing is derived from speech (de Saussure's position), but that code exceeds both in addressing both humans and machines. She is drawn more to the technological materialism of Kittler and his attention to the detail of code, with his insistence on the central importance of changes in voltage, treating signifiers as voltages and the signified as "interpretations that other layers of code give these voltages."[60] Further layers of translation from machine code to higher-level languages result in a chain of relations between signifier and signified based on the ability of the machine to recognize the difference between zero and one. Hayles considers code to determine actions with little ambiguity, although she does admit to the existence of noise with higher-level languages. For her purpose, she has problems with de Saussure's "dematerialized view of speech" and Derrida's "linguistic indeterminacy,"[61] as neither seems adequate to describe computational processes and actions. Yet what Hayles appears to overlook,

in her reliance on Kittler's technomaterialism, is her earlier insistence that machines
have bodies too. If code undermines the distinctions between speech and writing and
exceeds them, it is because it is a special kind of human-machine writing that makes
things happen; in other words, it acts like speech.

Speech act

In addition to the work of Searle and Wittgenstein, "speech act theory" derives from
John Langshaw Austin's *How to Do Things with Words* (1955), delivered as a series of
lectures examining ordinary linguistic usage and utterances.[62] In the first lecture,
Austin establishes that as well as providing descriptions, questions, and commands,
sentences can do something as opposed to just saying something: "to utter the sentence . . . is not to *describe* my doing of what I should be said in so uttering to be
doing or to state that I am doing it: it is to do it."[63] A sentence or utterance of this
type he calls a "performative," to indicate how it performs an action. In addition,
Austin introduces the term "operative" to indicate how saying something can make
it happen, as for instance in the practice of law, where an utterance serves to make
an instrumental effect.

His concern was to examine in what ways to say something is to do something,
how *in* saying something we do something, and how *by* saying something we do
something. In saying something, Austin writes, we may perform "locutionary acts"
(in providing the meaning of something, thus making a certain reference to something), "illocutionary acts" (in saying something with a certain force, such as inform-
ing, ordering, warning), and "perlocutionary acts" (in achieving certain effects by
saying something, such as persuading someone of something), among other types.[64]
The perlocutionary act marks a distinction between the action and its consequences,
and in this sense the consequences almost become the act itself, as with the following
example in which a light exists as a diode built into the hinge of a laptop, to inform
us of computational activity. By entering the operating system via the command line
interface, the program represents the light as a file, and when it sends the string "0
blink" to that file, the light flashes. In this sense, it speaks through the file to the
light.

```
# In the assertion "I speak,"
# I do something by saying these words;
# moreover, I declare what it is I do while I do it
echo "0 blink" > /proc/acpi/*/led # flash a light
```

Speech acts come close to the way program code performs an action, like the
instruction addressing the file. Programs are operative inasmuch as they do what they
say, but moreover they do what they say at the moment of saying it. What distin-
guishes the illocutionary act is that it is the very action that makes an effect: it says

and does what it says at the same time. Such utterances are not conventional but *performative*. In the analogy to code, what becomes useful is the recognition that speech produces an enormous variety of articulations that resist computational analysis, as described in the previous section. As the many attempts to build speech machines also indicate, speech is highly complex and not simply reducible to instrumental techniques and algorithms. The physiognomy of breath and muscle control, the tongue, lips, and larynx, and other cultural factors of language and dialect all add to the difficulty of simulation. Any spoken utterance is always locutionary in that it is an act of saying certain words, and of making movements with vocal cords and breath. Human gestures, such as those made by hands (aside from sign languages), can also be considered performative speech acts.[65] Adding a prosodic inflection to speech can give it a totally different meaning, perhaps only intended for certain listeners or contexts. There is necessarily a connection between saying something and physical action in a general sense. However, actions do not happen simply as a consequence of locution, as these further depend on outside factors.

Vocable Synthesis

Citing Schwitters's *Ursonate* as inspiration, Alex McLean's *Vocable Synthesis* (2008) is a system for improvising polymetric rhythms with vocable sounds.[66] He refers to the common use of vocable words in various musical traditions too: words (whether written, spoken, or sung) that are used for their sounds but not for wider meaning production. Vocables may be used to describe sounds, for example in the *bol* syllables of Indian classical music and the chanting or "mouth music" of the *canntaireachd*, the ancient Gaelic method of notating classical bagpipe music. Although far from standardized, *canntaireachd* operates through a combination of definite syllables (vowels represent the notes and consonants the embellishments, but this is not always the case) to enable the learner to recollect the tunes and easily transmit them orally. The following example of written *canntaireachd* is the ground (*urlar*) of *The Cave of Gold*, attributed to Donald Mor MacCrimmon, circa 1610:

Heinbodrie heunbodro, heinbodrie bitri betre, heinbodrie heunbodro, heinbetre odrierarierin, (repeat)
Heinbitri hereinve, heinbodro heororo, heinbitri hereinve, heinbetre odrierarierin,
Heinbitri hereinve, heinbodro heororo, heinbodrie heunbodro, heinbetre odrierarierin.[67]

In *Vocable Synthesis*, the sequence of letters making up a word is translated to a sequence of movements within a simulation of a drumstick hitting a drum skin. For example, the vocable word *kopatu* translates to "Hit loose, dampened drum outwards with heavy stiff mallet, then hit the middle of the drum with a lighter mallet while tightening the skin slightly and finally hit the edge of the skin with the same light mallet while loosening and releasing the dampening."[68] With vocable symbols, the idea is that the user/performer relates complex movements to his or her own voice, and therefore is arguably better able to intuitively understand and manipulate them musically. In this sense, the symbols speak to us. Below is an example session from the logs of *Babble* (2008),[69] an online version of *Vocable Synthesis*, showing a common pattern of the user writing text which, in response to the unconventional sounds that result, degrades through a series of edits into nonlexical rhythmic structure. As with *canntaireachd*, the idea is that the user is able to relate this to their voice, and therefore to intuitively understand and manipulate the symbols.

hola tarola
you don't know but that's ok, you might find me anyway
ooooooo uuu uiuiuu aeaeaee youaeae
olololololoo ululu uiluilulu alelalealele ylolulalelale

The user interface for *Vocable Synthesis* is built upon the GNU Readline library that allows editing of text in the UNIX command line (and its writerly qualities). The performer types a rhythm as a line of text, rather like a score for sound poetry. The sound itself is rather difficult to describe; you have to hear it—and of course it is performed in real time, like *Ursonate* itself. The program performs; and this is better considered to be a performative utterance or articulation, as it is not merely a demonstration of complex auditory signals. Through the analogy to speech, some core issues are also expressed that have been discussed in the chapter thus far, such as the poetic aspects of code and the ways humans communicate their understanding of code in terms of conversational forms and through social relations,[70] not least when it is performed as part of a live-coding event.

Excess

Although programming languages are clearly not spoken as such, they express particular qualities that come close to speech and even extend our understanding of speech. Computer code has both a legible state and an executable state, namely both readable and writable states at the level of language itself. This is precisely the point to stress in considering code for its speechlike qualities. The act of coding might be seen as the translation between a problem expressed in human terms of speech and one expressed in a way the computer can interpret, between ambiguous and complex expression and formal logic—or between loose and strict thinking. Clearly, performative utterances are linked to actions in a general sense, but, following Austin, it is interesting to think about how utterances express an internal act, almost like an intention to act: "the outward appearance is a description, true or false, of the occurrence of the inward performance."[71] Yet the force of the utterance is only understood in the context of its totality, the "total speech situation" as Austin calls it, inasmuch as it exceeds itself. This is not simply a question of understanding the context of the speech but of its excess, where context is lost or turns in on itself recursively.[72]

Confronting the notion that machines merely do what they are programmed to do, the understanding of programming as a performative speech act extends the unstable relation between the activities of writing, compiling, and running of code as a set of interconnected actions (as the practice of live coding demonstrates so well). Indeed, saying words or running code or simply understanding how they work is not enough in itself. What is important is the relation to the consequences of that action, and that is why the analogy of speech works especially well—although ultimately the phrase "speech act" may not be sufficient for the purpose.[73]

The various attempts to capture the voice in speech machines and software reveal the futility of the endeavor. In resisting the forces of rationality, it challenges normative communication and synthetic technologies of the general economy, resonating more with the notion of excess.[74] That the voice cannot be fully captured by computation is very much the point, as it provides inspiration for new ways of working with code and examining "code acts," to reveal other possibilities and motivations.

2   Code Working

The phrase "code working" draws attention to the work involved in writing code, as well as the work that code does once executed. If physical, intellectual, and machine labor have become less and less differentiated, as labor has become more immaterial, collective, and communicative,[1] then labor's performative and linguistic (speechlike) qualities also require new emphasis. The workings of code encapsulate these qualities, not least in recognition that work is increasingly practiced at the behest of scripts.

The chapter emphasizes the cultural materiality of working with code, insofar as all codework necessarily carries with it the labor that has been invested in its production, as well as the labor invested in the broader apparatuses through which it is served. The code artist Alan Sondheim summarizes the relations of production in coding and its potential to reveal hidden layers of operation: "Every more or less traditional text is codework with invisible residue; every computer harbors the machinic, the ideology of capital in the construction of its components, the oppression of underdevelopment in its reliance on cheap labor."[2] Indeed, one should not underestimate how much software development is outsourced to software houses in parts of the world where labor comes cheap. The trick, on both global and local levels, is to hide the code content and coding labor under a deceptive rhetorical form, rather than reveal the contradictions of value and hence divisions of labor involved in production. Therefore the discussion of work in this chapter is allied to coding in a deliberately ambiguous way, to indicate the work involved in making software as well as the work that software does itself (in parallel to the way that speech both says and does something at the same time). These comments apply to cultural and artistic work in particular, inasmuch as this is where the software and the work of the programmer combine with hardware in performative ways. This indicates a conceptual turn in the consideration and practice of coding work, as work has become more identified with intellectual endeavor and linguistic competence. The point is that the very contradictions of labor value are encoded in ever more complex ways, through "machinic" social relations that involve humans *and* machines, and activities related to the networked extensions of the body and the intellect.[3]

A familiar line of argument describes how commercial software closes off the source code that the programmer works with, and thus makes its workings relatively inaccessible to further use or indeed criticism. The proprietary software compiles the code into an executable version that locks down the source, offering a useful analogy to the ways in which capital protects its interests. In response to this, many software producers have made the source code an integral part of the work, quite literally in their production of codeworks (as for instance with Harwood's *Perl Routines to Manipulate London*, cited in the previous chapter). Thus it becomes possible for codeworks to reveal some of the contradictions over production involved in working with code, in parallel to labor conditions and class struggle more broadly. Harwood's codework *Class Library* (2008) plays on these inherent antagonisms, along with the double coding of the term "class."[4] Below is a short extract:

```
package DONT::CARE;
use strict; use warnings;
sub aspire {
my $class{tab}          = POOR;
my $requested_type      = GET_RICHER;
my $aspiration{tab}     = "$requested_type.pm";
my $class{tab}          = "POOR::$requested_type";
require $aspiration;
return $class->new(@_);
}
1;
```

Evidently an understanding of work can be developed that takes account of the dynamic character of social processes, using secondary notation to form arguments as well as the internal contradictions that are evident in code itself. New contradictions are expressed in the complexity of coding labor relations, characterized not least by the production of free software and open licenses, which rely on the sharing of source code and expertise. The chapter elaborates on these issues and the paradoxes that arise, to demonstrate how the practice of coding extends social relations from the basic interaction of workers to their interactions with machines and code. It addresses the question of how working with code relates to work and action, firstly by discussing the ways that new ideas emerge through the loops of historical processes.

The dynamic relation between code and the actions that arise from it are an indication of wider recursive processes. The second section of the chapter considers how work has incorporated the communicative and linguistic dimension, facilitated by networked technologies and collective formations of work that together can be understood through the concept of "general intellect" (taken from the "Fragment on Machines" in Marx's *Grundrisse*).[5] The concept indicates the productive connection between networked machines and collective human intelligence, or what might be more usefully referred to here as networked intelligence, materialized in software practices that share code. The final section develops ideas of codework more specifically in relation to Arendt's distinctions between work and action,[6] to dispute deterministic ideas that program code is simply a means to an end (its functional application), or an end without means (necessarily closed off, locked down by commercial imperatives). Something far more paradoxical is offered, informed by artistic and other idiosyncratic interventions. Underlying the chapter as a whole is an exploration of the conditions on which labor relations are based, speculating on the possibility of work and code operating for-themselves in a speechlike manner.

Code in-itself

If coding is simultaneously saying something and doing it, what came before? Clearly someone conceives the program, as indicated by the etymology of the word "program" from the Greek *programma*, a written notice to the public. It indicates a procedural way of doing things, which is important for understanding computational processes more broadly: the logic of "*if* something *then* something else," for instance. As a noun, "program" is a description of a future event and a set of instructions used to execute a specified task. As a verb, it describes the process of the arrangement of the program as the expression but also the operation of the computer or machine in executing the instructions. The procedure is also ideological, as computational processes operate like other rhetorical strategies, something that Ian Bogost's phrase "procedural rhetoric" makes clear in describing how computational processes (like good speeches) model persuasion in systems involving the interpretation of any symbolic system that governs thinking and action[7]—between sender and receiver, speaker and listener, writer and reader, programmer and user.

In such ways, analogies can be drawn between the temporal operations of programming and historical processes more broadly.[8] For example, the codework *Repeating History* (2009) by Pall Thayer emphasizes that historical processes are not linear but cyclic. Significantly, it is also released for further modification and comes with the warning that if the script is run, it could cause damage to the user's system.[9]

```
#!/usr/bin/perl
sub relive {$command = shift;print `$command`;}
$bash_history = $ENV{ HOME }."/.bash_history";
while(1){
  open(HISTORY, $bash_history);
  while($moment = <HISTORY>){
    relive($moment);
  }
}
```

As evident if it is run, the source code expresses both what it will do and what it can do at the same time—like history, its operations can be thought of as relays between what exists and what is possible. Stretching the analogy further, it can be argued that the programmer is not simply doing work that becomes the object of history but intervening in the very processes of history. This evokes a position informed by historical materialism, that there are social forces that intervene in the process of history, and that humans and their ideas take an active role in this process. This is what Marx was referring to in "The Eighteenth Brumaire of Louis Bonaparte" (1852) when he claimed: "Men make their own history, but they do not make it as they please; they do not make it under self-selected circumstances, but under circumstances existing already, given and transmitted from the past. The tradition of all dead generations weighs like a nightmare on the brains of the living."[10] In historical materialist thinking, this fact underpins antagonistic relations (like the class anger expressed in Harwood's codework) as the subject gains self-knowledge of his or her role in history. However, the view that human subjects make their own history, even under particular circumstances, is now considered far too deterministic (and unfortunately seems to have been disproven by history), and agency is widely recognized as far more contingent on external conditions than simply preprogrammed in human subjectivity.[11]

Does this mean we are free agents only in the sense that we do not recognize the determining factors that control us? This goes some way to describe the gap between our lived sense of reality and what precedes it, forever bound into paradoxical relations. To Hegel, this logic indicated the passage from being "in-itself" (in its essence) to "for-itself" (in actuality), later adapted by Marx to describe the passage to class consciousness.[12] Acting for-itself seems to suggest something close to the operations of speech acts and program code, which are both preprogrammed to act and simply need to be executed. The question remains how to reconcile this rather deterministic view with broader contingencies.

Emergence

Historical processes can be understood as phenomena that are analogous to the inner workings of wider systems; they express ongoing processes of development and complexity, beyond the reach of a linear narrative of progress or the straightforward accumulation of knowledge.[13] Those keen to defend Hegel from the accusation of teleology (such as Žižek)[14] would suggest that his idea of the end of history has been misunderstood and that his approach is predicated on contingency and adaptive logic. The passage from in-itself to for-itself describes a developmental process in which consciousness of conditions is derived recursively, generating a consciousness of consciousness (as mind shapes the perception of the mind, echoing one of the principles of second-order cybernetics, or "cybernetics of cybernetics").[15] What appears is not true knowledge but what appears to be known, adding another level of consciousness, and so on, in an ongoing generative process. Moreover, the subject does not simply recognize false conditions nor is driven by a concept of preprogrammed subjectivity, but there is an antagonistic interaction of the two—combining both internal and external factors, oscillating between what is possible and what actually exists, but crucially without losing the antagonism between them. Žižek refers to this as "tarrying with the negative," the retention of contradiction rather than the creation of false totalities.[16] His point is that Hegel's conception, even though it tells a story about universal freedom, still allows for new historical departures, and thus remains useful.

Taking this adaptive logic a step further, critical realism (associated with Roy Bhaskar) aims to extend Hegelian thinking and to recognize the "emergent properties of the social realm."[17] Social phenomena can be seen to contain emergent properties as part of an open system that generates new possibilities. An understanding of adaptive systems informs this view, and also undermines any teleological or linear understanding of history (associated with Hegel and aspects of Marx in particular), making it far more recursive.[18] However, the dialectical concept of negation is not rejected but redefined as something more transformative, dynamic, and contingent.[19] Drawing on second-order cybernetics, Bhaskar describes the world as an open system, or more exactly as an "open-systemic entropic totality, in which results . . . are neither auto-genetically produced nor even constellationally closed, but the provisional outcome of a heterogeneous multiplicity of changing mechanisms, agencies and circumstances."[20] He conceptualizes agency similarly, in terms of incompleteness or insufficient totality that drives transformation. This is characterized by the concept "transformative agency," to stress the importance of ideas and the active role of people in historical development; and also to recognize that people do not simply make their own history nor are determined by history, but both: they both act and are acted upon. In other words, there is a feedback loop that describes the way the historical subject can reassemble itself or self-organize, in the passage from in-itself to for-itself.

Computation

What does an understanding of computational processes further contribute to this understanding of the relations between speech and code, if there is a recognition that the historical subject can both program and be programmed? In a history of computing, for instance, Charles Babbage's "Analytical Engine" (first described in 1837) extended the earlier "Difference Engine" (first conceived in 1786) by employing the principle of the "strange loop" or "tangled hierarchy," a mathematical theory describing the capability of a computer to alter its own stored program.[21] This logic is taken to an extreme in the case of code that is self-referential or recursive, such as a "quine," a term used to describe a program whose output is exactly the same as its complete source code. The idea is summarized by Hofstadter using quine as a verb, meaning, "to write (a sentence fragment) a first time, and then to write it a second time, but with quotation marks around it." For example, if we quine "say," we get "say 'say'."[22]

The "while loop" in programming allows sections of code to be repeated until a specified condition is met. In Alex McLean's artwork *forkbomb.pl* (2002),[23] one while loop is embedded in another, a technique often used for manipulating two-dimensional data. However, this construct is twisted in on itself by the final "goto" instruction which jumps back inside the loop, so that the two while statements are notionally inside each other. Stranger still, the "fork" instructions cause the process to split into two every time a while condition is tested, so that the condition simultaneously succeeds and fails in different processes. This also means that the number of processes doubles in every loop, quickly reaching the operating system's limits and possibly causing it to crash.

```
#!/usr/bin/perl

no warnings;

my $strength = $ARGV[0] + 1;
while (not fork) {
  exit unless --$strength;
  print 0;
  twist: while (fork) {
    exit unless --$strength;
    print 1;
  }
}
goto 'twist' if --$strength;
```

The script prints out zeros in the outer and ones in the inner while loop, which are shown in figure 2.1 as white and black pixels. Because *forkbomb.pl* pushes the system to its limits, it becomes sensitive to subtleties of timing and state in the operating system. For this reason the output is different every time it is run and the output is an artistic impression of your system under strain.

The way endless loops work on themselves—as if in self-recognition of wider conditions—neatly corresponds with a dialectical understanding of the inherent antagonism between internal and external factors, oscillating between what is possible and what actually exists. That the script "bombs" the system is also evocative in terms of wider critical expression, such as the adaptation to US foreign policy in *forkwar.pl* (2003), by deprogramming.us.[24]

Clearly, computational processes execute a very particular view of history, and the operations of memory and storage are key to this. In solving a given problem, the

Figure 2.1
Alex McLean, output of *forkbomb.pl* (2002).

central processor takes symbols from memory, combines or compares them with other symbols, and then restores them to memory. "Memory" here is random-access memory (RAM), where programs are created, loaded, and run in temporary storage; whether these are written to hard memory becomes an intriguing analogy for the ways in which memory is loaded into history (and how this process is ideological in terms of what becomes official history).[25] Perhaps the oral history tradition seems a less distorted version of events, as it involves less-mediated forms of history like the subjective realm of memory itself. Nevertheless, however inscribed, data is selected, stored, processed, and also deleted in all systems.[26]

History is full of such examples and can be understood in similar terms of storage and deletion, turning human intelligence into artificial intelligence and producing artificial history. With the shortcomings of artificial intelligence in mind,[27] an important and recurring reference is the machine built by Wolfgang von Kempelen in 1769—a chess-playing automaton dressed in Turkish attire that wins every time it plays—which introduces Walter Benjamin's essay "On the Concept of History."[28] In the terms of the essay, the example of Kempelen's automaton, well known in Benjamin's time, demonstrates that the dynamic of history (like that of the machine) is

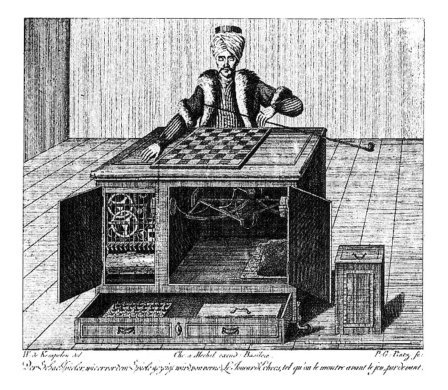

Figure 2.2
Wolfgang von Kempelen, *The Turk*, also known as the *Mechanical Turk* or *Automaton Chess Player* (1769). Copper engraving from Karl Gottlieb von Windisch's *Briefe über den Schachspieler des Hrn. von Kempelen, nebst drei Kupferstichen die diese berühmte Maschine vorstellen* (1783). Image in public domain.

fake; the task of the historical materialist is to reveal the inner workings as ideological constructions, so that they can be further modified.

Whether this machine was driven by magic or by some other (Orientalist) trickery that made it able to play chess so well was a subject of much public discussion. Despite the apparatus being "stripped naked" as part of the presentation, the accepted historical view is that a small person was hidden under the automaton's table and operated the chess pieces through the use of magnets.[29] The controversy continued when Edgar Allan Poe compared the chess automaton to Babbage's calculating machine, questioning the authenticity of machines "without any immediate human agency."[30] For Benjamin this is exactly the point, and moreover that the illusions are challenged by the expertise embedded within; the forces that guide the puppet's hand by means of strings, like its counterpart historical materialism, are such that it always wins.

Voice

To Dolar, there is a further aspect of the ghost in the machine, namely the voice.[31] He refers to another invention by Kempelen, his speech machine of 1780 (mentioned in the previous chapter), and the way the voice is tied to subjectivity and to the unconscious, whereas with the chess-playing machine the link is between subjectivity and the appearance of intelligence (or consciousness). Actually the two examples are even more connected, as, after Kempelen's death, Johan Nepomuk Maelsel added some improvements to the chess-playing machine including speech—the announcement of "échec" (check) by means of bellows—to further authenticate its apparent "intelligence." Jonathan Rée also comments on the chess-playing machine, suggesting a media-archaeological approach to the role of artificial speech in relation to speech as the source of human society and history. Rée cites examples of how the analysis of speech informed the development of other media forms, such as the early description of cinema as "speech photography"; many of the examples from the previous chapter might also support such an approach that associates speech with authenticity.[32]

The distinction between the two Kempelen machines is quite precise for Dolar, who applies the Hegelian formulation: we move from "in-itself" in the case of the speaking machine to "for-itself" in the thinking machine.[33] Speech is the hidden mechanism behind thought, like the puppet in the chess-playing automaton or the ghost in the machine. Dolar proposes that Benjamin's conclusion be modified, such that "if the puppet called historical materialism is to win, it should enlist the services of the voice."[34] In similar ways, recognition of the layers of code could also be of service in disputing surface appearances, and in this way human subjects may be in a better position to modify their circumstances if they enlist the services of technical expertise and collective labor related to code. Thus it might become possible to conceive of software operating for-itself, in recognition of the complexities of the work, action, and intellect embedded in its forms.

Coding work

How has work itself transformed and incorporated the communicative dimension, making all work more like codework? The general claim is that the living contradiction of labor relations in the factory has been extended by collectivity and connectivity to the "social factory."[35] The figure of the factory remains useful to reinforce the view that all social relationships lie in social production and relationships between people in production, but these conditions have been extended more widely into society. In orthodox Marxism, the capitalist mode of production simultaneously produces and reproduces the antagonistic social relations between labor and capital contained within the site of production. But labor is no longer simply contained by

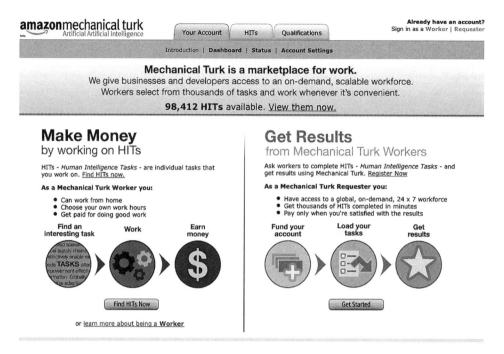

Figure 2.3
Amazon Mechanical Turk's homepage (2011). Screenshot.

the factory walls, as part of a process that Marx termed "real subsumption" (in *Grundrisse*) to conceptualize the way class exploitation is subsumed into the wider social realm.[36] This is clearly more evident under contemporary conditions than it was in the mid-nineteenth century, as the process of subsumption is now assisted by informational technologies and networked intelligence.

Amazon's Mechanical Turk is a case in point. Intriguingly named after Kempelen's automaton, it is an online marketplace for precarious work, running since 2005. It does not hide the labor of the worker but celebrates its immaterial character. Using so-called "artificial artificial intelligence,"[37] it claims to provide a marketplace for work, "to give businesses and developers access to an on-demand, scalable workforce," so that "Human Intelligence Tasks" can be executed (although some tasks, it acknowledges, are performed better by humans than machines). At the same time, and for obvious reasons, labor relations are downplayed through carefully chosen language, describing "requesters" rather than employers, perhaps to avoid questions of labor value and subsequent antagonisms. Even more depressing is that so-called "Turkers" in the US use this "crowdsourcing marketplace" as a form of entertainment. As Trebor Scholz puts it, "The biggest trick that Mechanical Turk ever pulled off was to make

Figure 2.4
Aaron Koblin, *The Sheep Market* (2006). Image courtesy of Aaron Koblin.

workers believe that what they do is not really work. That, at least, is somewhat suggested by the slogan on MTurk's coffee mugs: 'Why work if you can turk?'"[38]

Artists have also enthusiastically responded with experiments in crowdsourcing, such as Aaron Koblin's *The Sheep Market* (2006), a collection of 10,000 sheep made by workers using Mechanical Turk, each paid US$0.02 to "draw a sheep facing to the left."[39] Whether effective irony or not, such examples reflect how labor is becoming ever more informational and communicative, leading to a situation in which all activities seem to have been turned into production.[40] *The Sheep Market* is also a good example of how capital tries to capture the creative and communicative capacity of the socialized labor force and turn it into information that can be marketized.

Consequently, the site of antagonisms has been extended to include the control of communications and the labor related to communications; the struggle is no longer simply between workers and capitalists but also between communities and platforms (which the following chapter will discuss in more detail through an engagement with more public forms). Class antagonism is transformed into a broader dynamic, as a consequence of the collapse of the management of production and the action of production itself, between conception and execution, exploding the site of conflict to society as a whole. Following this line of thought, neither labor time nor wage is considered to be the central issue under critique but technological skill and organizational forms defined by cultural, informational factors and knowledge. Productive labor is upgraded by intellectual, immaterial, and communicative labor, disrupting orthodox conceptions of labor, value, and agency.[41] Work is reconnected to and extracted from the body, mind, and soul.

Valorization

In *The Soul at Work*, Berardi examines these contemporary forms that put the soul to work, taking his cue from Spinoza (taking the soul, in other words, in a materialist sense, not related to religion as such).[42] Berardi insists on a shift of attention to the way contemporary modes of production convert mind, language, and creativity (together taken to be attributes of the soul) into value. Therefore these combined territories of the intellect, language, and imagination become core concerns for understanding contemporary forms of alienation, as the soul is no longer ignored but directly engaged, with alienation now extended to the whole of life. To understand alienation, he charts its passage from the Hegelian-Marxist tradition—where it is measured between human essence and the perversion of this into work activity, the split between life and labor (close to Arendt's distinctions to be taken up later in the chapter)—to the Italian workerist tradition where it is defined in relation to labor time and the creation of value, "the reification of body and soul," as Berardi puts it.[43]

The significance of the break represented by workerism (and later Autonomia) is the rejection of the passivity of the worker and insistence on the possibilities of active "refusal of work," as a strategy of exit from the capitalist valorization process.[44] This tactic is based on the paradox that Mario Tronti's essay "The Strategy of Refusal" identified in 1965: that the logic of capital "seeks to use the worker's antagonistic will-to-struggle as a motor for its own development."[45] The paradox is that capital does not wish to destroy critique but tame it through processes of subsumption. Berardi's genealogy of alienation demonstrates how antagonism in the refusal of work has moved to a situation where work increasingly seems to define subjectivities, all aspects and every detail of life, the very essence of the living thing (and this is what constitutes the soul according to Aristotle).[46] In integrating intellect, language, and imagination, labor power produces new and more totalizing kinds of subjectivities. What Berardi refers to as the soul—and for the argument here, the voice—are now also deeply implicated in these processes.

Networked communication technologies play a significant role in these processes of subjectification as they relate to general intellect, forming networked intelligence.[47] With this concept (an elaboration of subsumption), already Marx had predicted that the productive forces of the intellect, of human knowledge and skills, would be incorporated into capital itself. The crucial issue, both then and now, is that general intellect

unleashes contradictions by combining technical knowledge and the social cooperation of bodies. The concept is somewhat materialized in the procedures of Amazon's
Mechanical Turk and more generally in coding cultures, where connectivity is reflected
in the open-source and free software movements as an example of how technical
expertise and socialized labor can be shared and recombined effectively. Such ways of
working with software are arguably more robust and less bug-ridden as a result of
collective development, but the contradictions are also evident, as this approach
becomes the orthodoxy in the release of proprietary software development too. Indeed
free and open software principles both contest and affirm capital investment on
human and economic levels, as labor expands to involve cultural activities not tradi-
tionally considered to constitute work, including intellectual labor and artistic practices.[48] Indeed, the once straightforward distinction between waged and unwaged
work, or work and nonwork (play), becomes ever harder to establish.

If the complexities of contemporary labor are exemplified by the ways in which
waged and free labor have become harder to differentiate, much is also now practiced
outside of traditional production processes, on computers and across telecommunica-
tion networks. The former distinction between leisure time and work time is now
further confused by the ways physical labor, intellectual labor, and machine labor have
collapsed in on themselves. Consequently, a traditional view of labor value appears
inadequate because of the difficulty in calculating working time related to signification, as opposed to the relative ease of calculating working time in making traditional
material goods. To Tiziana Terranova, the complexities of contemporary labor value
are characterized by free labor within capitalism, rather than by gift economies and
systems of exchange in societies outside its reach.[49] Therefore the production of free
and open-source software cannot be considered to be an alternative to capitalism but
an expression of new forms of labor within capitalism, "part of the process of economic experimentation with the creation of monetary value out of knowledge/culture/
affect."[50]

What is considered "free," whether labor, software, or speech, is clearly based upon
market infrastructures that use intellectual property rights to further vested interests.
Free speech operates with similar paradoxes (discussed in more detail in the following
chapter), since ideas are no longer free once made tangible. This is a by-product of
neoliberalism that tries to capture all forms of labor, including intellectual labor and
protest. But although capital tries to treat ideas as it would any other goods, it does
not succeed in commodifying them altogether, because intellectual work is not simply
reducible to market principles. This is a point that Maurizio Lazzarato makes in relation to books, drawing on the work of the sociologist Gabriel Tarde to explain that
the market can only determine a book's exchange value as a product, not its value as
knowledge.[51] In a similar way, the publishing of books can be understood as an attempt
to commodify the oral tradition of storytelling.

Property

Similar ambiguities apply to artistic works in general, and especially to those that follow a conceptual tradition or are performed live or involve speech, as the legal apparatus struggles to adapt to informational logic and remains locked into frameworks that tend to consider tangible objects rather than intangible ideas. So too with codework, and perhaps especially so when it is in the public domain.

An example that played on these ambiguities was Robert Luxembourg's *The Conceptual Crisis of Private Property as a Crisis in Practice* (2003), which consisted of program code (crisis.php), an explanatory text file (crisis.txt), and a screenshot (crisis.png).[52] If the program was run, it parsed the screenshot into the full text of the novel *Cryptonomicon* by Neal Stephenson (of 1999). The project operated as a conceptual puzzle that contained a number of interconnected parts all found in the screenshot itself. These included a still from the film *The Matrix*,[53] and a passage from Hardt and Negri's *Empire* (published in 2000) that questioned the limits of the legal apparatus that underpins contemporary power structures[54] (and this passage from Hardt and Negri also supplies the phrase that Robert Luxembourg uses for his work's title). The project thus formed a neat conceptual loop about encryption and intellectual property rights, allowing readers to gain access to the Stephenson book and at the same time for the author of the software to notionally circumvent the legal constraints imposed by the publishers. The conceit was that the script does not infringe copyright in itself, but only if executed by the user.[55]

Apart from being a novel about encryption, it is also interesting to note that *Cryptonomicon* demonstrates the interactions of code and written text languages, as Stephenson is both a print author and a computer programmer. It follows that it can be read as both written text and a program to be executed in its reading, evoking his nonfiction work *In the Beginning Was the Command Line* that charts his migration from Macintosh to UNIX-based operating systems (written 1995–1998, simultaneous to *Cryptonomicon*). The fact that the GNU General Public License agreement emerged from a UNIX culture of sharing also sets the release of the crisis.php script in sharp contrast to the constrained conditions of distribution of the book it de-encypts.

The various licenses on offer to software producers reflect the ways that code as an intangible object is being forced into a property regime by those who wish to consider it to be like any other material goods that can be traded in the open market. The perversity of the logic is the basis for Stallman's argument in "Why Software Should Not Have Owners," and his position that to think of software in these terms and to adopt their legal protections is anachronistic.[56] The legal apparatus remains poorly suited to dealing with the results of immaterial labor, as it still tends to view property in terms of end products and is unable to deal with other modes of production, such as commons-based production (more on this issue will be developed in the following chapter). Open license agreements, such as those provided by the Creative Commons

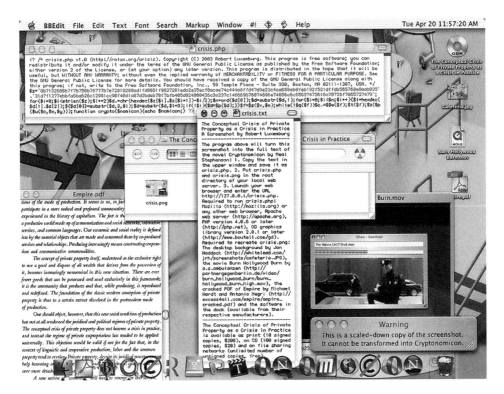

Figure 2.5
Robert Luxembourg, *The Conceptual Crisis of Private Property as a Crisis in Practice* (2003).
Screenshot.

initiative, may be useful in providing flexible copyright licenses for creative works, but they do not adequately address the problem at the site of production.[57] Indeed, as many commentators have pointed out, they arguably represent the potential for the further commodification of the creative work invested in the first place.[58] Even the more radical Creative Commons "Public Domain Dedication, No Copyright" license speaks the language of law: "The person who associated a work with this deed has *dedicated* the work to the public domain by waiving all of his or her rights to the work worldwide under copyright law, including all related and neighboring rights, to the extent allowed by law. You can copy, modify, distribute and perform the work, even for commercial purposes, all without asking permission."[59]

If the legal apparatus, ironically itself a performative language, sets out to turn information into commodities, then alternatives are required that seek to free ideas from their complicity with these constraints. An extreme position is to reject copyright altogether, following the logic that any form of property rights over the commons is unethical. This is the position taken by Piratbyrån (the bureau of piracy), the founders of the peer-to-peer bittorrent site Pirate Bay, when they reject copyright with the slogan "No copyright. No license,"[60] or by using the imperative "Copy Me!"[61] The more pragmatic and alternative critique provided by copyleft licenses (GPL being the earliest example, in 1989) maintains the right to copy and share enshrined in the legal apparatus; although such licenses may go further than Creative Commons, they still serve to reinforce the system of copyright, even through its apparent negation.

In the "copyfarleft" license, Dmytri Kleiner takes copyleft further by addressing some of the problems associated with the expropriation of free labor, in arguing for licenses combined with class consciousness. He states: "While copyleft is very effective in creating a commons of software, to achieve a commons of cultural works requires copyfarleft, a form of free licensing that denies free access to organizations that hold their own assets outside the commons."[62] His position, in keeping with the title of his book *The Telekommunist Manifesto,* is that the rejection of property regimes is only possible once a classless society has been achieved; for the system of property itself needs to be further negated if one follows the Hegelian notion of "negation of negation" (which would regard an initial negation of copyleft as still operating with the symbolic confines of property, and hence its further negation as necessary to account for external conditions).[63]

One of the political challenges is to apply copyleft thinking more generally to tangible goods, not the other way around, as the legal apparatus attempts. Kleiner develops analogies between technical and social systems of organization in a section of his book called "Peer-to-Peer Communism vs The Client-Server Capitalist State," where distributed forms like the commons are contrasted with centralized statist forms.[64] He identifies the contradiction at the core of free culture with its connection to the term "free market," which is clearly not free but a description of the market economy that follows "unfree" principles. The concept of economic rent is used to indicate the income that owners earn simply from the act of ownership itself,[65] like the earnings derived by "landlords" letting private property (the name comes from the enclosure of common land by lords). Both capitalist and landlord expropriate in this way. What is developed in terms of this critique is that property remains a core issue, enshrined in the legal apparatus to protect class divisions and to legitimize rent.

If the law is a speech act, then perhaps the whole legal system needs to be negated through language, destabilizing its codes. Virno's nondialectical understanding of negation refers to the inherent paradoxes of language as it both does negation (by identifying what something is not) and is negation (inasmuch as it can only signify something).[66] More will be said of this in the last chapter, but for now it suggests possibilities for new "nonrepresentational" forms of political organization that are based on speech acts that adhere to distributed forms and common ownership.

Self-organization

The political point is that ownership should apply to labor, not property. "Venture communism" is the ironic term Kleiner uses to evoke workers' self-organization, to address the way that class conflict is conceived across telecommunications networks through the pervasive use of Internet and mobile technologies. This becomes the foundation for a critique of the rise of social media in particular as a project of venture capitalism that expropriates developments in the free software movement and commons-based peer-to-peer technologies.[67] The point remains that ownership and property are core issues in these platforms; they are organized in ways that follow the logic of rent, to secure profit from immaterial assets. The owners profit through centralized control, whereas the distinctiveness of peer production lies in the relative independence of workers to control common productive assets and share the benefits. The idea of venture communism registers the need to develop an alternative business model that supports these principles, and at the same time rejects the way that value has been stolen from the commons in the first place.

An example of software that attempts to apply this logic is *Thimbl* (2010–2011), a free, open-source, distributed microblogging platform developed by the Telekommunisten collective (of which Kleiner is a founding member). The publicity on the website confirms: "The most significant challenge the open web will need to overcome is not technical, it is political."[68] *Thimbl* uses a common server software called Finger, adapted to the principles of the open web, and positions it in relation to the legacy of peer-to-peer organizational forms such as UseNet (the distributed messaging system, operating since 1979 although since subsumed by the Google monopoly).[69] This reflects one of Kleiner's main arguments, that social networking with its participatory ethic has been largely stolen from free software development, a theft interpreted as "capitalism's pre-emptive attack against peer-to-peer systems."[70]

The history of *Thimbl*'s technical development is important of course, and political in terms of its negation of dominant infrastructure: unlike a platform like Twitter, where the service is provided through a client-server architecture, with *Thimbl* clients are encouraged to become active in their co-ownership of the service with other "workers." Yet this is largely a symbolic gesture, not a viable alternative to Twitter as such but a performative artwork, or "performative science fiction" as Kleiner puts it.[71] He also clarifies that the speculation is not based on technical viability, as it does work, but more on economic viability, exemplifying the concept of venture communism: "Thimbl is an economic fiction."[72] Based on an understanding of the political economy of social media, its intention is to uncover uneven social relations embedded in communication technology, creating a platform that works in unexpected ways, like other projects of Telekommunisten's Miscommunication Technologies series.[73]

In this way, the ability to use technology differently can still be seen to rest with those who have the expertise to operate it; not the platform owners or landlords, but

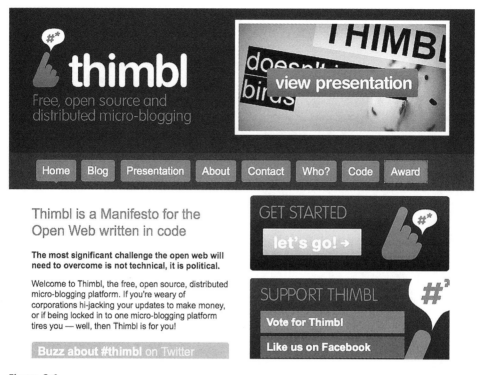

Figure 2.6
Telekommunisten, *Thimbl* (2010–2011). Screenshot of homepage. Image courtesy of Telekommunisten.

the software developers, systems operators, programmers, technicians, office workers, designers, artists, and so on. Given this emphasis, it is work itself that needs to be transformed and made more autonomous. It follows that new collective characterizations are required that respond to both social cooperation and technical knowledge, and the threat posed by market forces in striving to capture networked intelligence.

The unstable relations within sociotechnical systems between human and machine labor indicate some of the possibilities for rethinking the social relations of production in working with code and being worked on by code. Another precedent for this line of argument lies in Félix Guattari's comment in *Chaosophy* that Marx was mistaken in thinking social relations lie outside of the tool and the machine.[74] The distinction between tool and machine is much misunderstood, and often further confused in connection with software and hardware. To clarify, Marx stressed that machines are a factor of communication, whereas tools merely extend control through direct contact: "the tool is a simple machine and the machine is a complex tool."[75] The machine becomes more and more independent of the worker, extending the limits of human effort, and becomes part of a wider scheme of machines working together collectively: "Here we have, in place of the isolated machine, a mechanical monster whose body fills whole factories, and whose demonic power, at first hidden by the slow and measured motions of its gigantic members, finally bursts forth in the fast and feverish whirl of its countless working organs."[76]

The worker too becomes ever more like a machine, prefigured in the development of automata and "second-order robots" programming their sequences of work. But the complex relations of worker and machine, prefigured in the rhetorical descriptions of factories as giant automata or workers as robots,[77] requires further elaboration, as worker and tool are part of ever more expansive machinic assemblages.[78] To explain: the writing, compiling, and running code are part of software that, along with hardware and with the labor invested in both, makes the computer-machine assemblage as a whole. So rather than the dead labor of machines replacing human labor, or other simplifications, Guattari states: "On the contrary, I think that machines must be used—and all kinds of machines, whether concrete or abstract, technical, scientific or artistic. Machines do more than revolutionize the world, they completely recreate it."[79]

The argument of this section has been to consider work in these machinic terms, to look beyond the emancipatory rhetoric of free software to a more detailed understanding of labor and agency across a plurality of social movements, worker self-organization, and coding cultures, and the ability to write, compile, and run code in unexpected ways. *Ungovernable.patch* details a small change to the Linux kernel, in the standard "patch" format that programmers use to share modifications to software. The change alters the working behavior of the "governor," the operating system component that changes the speed of the computer processor. Instead of making the computer operate faster when there is more work to do, it works faster when there is *less* to do. The human is forced to work in cooperation with the machine, finding that the computer quickly tires if too much is asked of it but works very well in response to less demanding tasks.

```
# ungovernable.patch (c) 2011, released under the GPL version 2
--- vanilla/drivers/cpufreq/cpufreq_ondemand.c
+++ new/drivers/cpufreq/cpufreq_ondemand.c
@@ -494,7 +494,7 @@
    }

    /* Check for frequency increase */
-   if (max_load_freq > dbs_tuners_ins.up_threshold * policy->cur) {
+   if (max_load_freq <= dbs_tuners_ins.up_threshold * policy->cur) {
      /* If switching to max speed, apply sampling_down_factor */
     if (policy->cur < policy->max)
        this_dbs_info->rate_mult =
@@ -513,7 +513,7 @@
```

```
     * can support the current CPU usage without triggering the up
     * policy. To be safe, we focus 10 points under the threshold.
     */
-    if (max_load_freq <
+    if (max_load_freq >=
        (dbs_tuners_ins.up_threshold - dbs_tuners_ins.down_differential) *
        policy->cur) {
          unsigned int freq_next;
```

Code action

If the concept of speech acts is one way of characterizing the breakdown of distinctions across the different articulations of code working, then more detail is required on the matter of execution (as the above example demonstrates to some degree). This last section of the chapter elaborates on the relationship of work to action, in order to respond to the changed relationship between conception and execution of work, enacted materially by instructions.

It begins from Arendt's essay of 1964, "Labor, Work, Action,"[80] in which she addresses the distinctions between these three terms and what she considered to be a problem in orthodox Marxist thinking, that labor was tied too firmly to work at the expense of action. Arendt's understanding of action is a critique of the Platonic separation of knowing and doing, in which knowledge is identified with command and action with execution. These ideas are evident in the process of fabrication, "first perceiving the image or shape (*eidos*) of the produce-to-be, and then organizing the means and starting the execution."[81] According to Arendt, the mistake involves substituting making for action (persistent in political theory in general, in the centrality of "production"), and this leads to a line of thought in which any means appear justifiable to pursue a recognized end. This is the instrumental logic of "you can't make an omelette without breaking eggs," as she puts it, in which ethical considerations are suspended.[82] In contrast, she insists that human action lies in the realm of uncertainty, as something that cannot be fully known and as part of an ongoing process of setting something in motion without an end in mind. Ideas are not simply executed but continually interpreted in real time.

This line of thought holds a number of implications for coding practices, and certainly the description of continual interpretation is consistent with computer processing, but first the terms "work" and "labor" require more definition if we are to understand making activities more generally.[83] According to Arendt, a basic distinction can be made between *homo faber*, who makes and works upon something or fabricates it, and *animal laborans*, which produces labor at the level of life itself (and provides salvation for the soul).[84] In *animal laborans*, the human body is given over to labor, evident in the reproductive processes in their broadest sense (the pains of birth are considered to be labor, for instance). Whereas labor combines production and consumption like life itself (and speech of course), the fabricated thing (as a result of work) is an end product, derived from a production process entirely separate from its possible uses (such as a book or software). These are categories of means and ends, and the significance is that certain "works" do not fit into the deterministic "means-end" chain of events.

Virtuosity

To Arendt, the work of art is both the most enduring and most useless fabricated object that human hands can produce: "the proper intercourse with a work of art is certainly not 'using' it; on the contrary, it must be removed carefully from the whole context of ordinary use objects to attain its proper place in the world."[85] This is a general observation, of course, and certainly much software production sits uneasily among her distinctions, but her main point is that the performative arts are particularly resistant to reification as the least materialistic of the arts.[86] Poetry too (especially if spoken) demonstrates procedures that are close to thought processes that have neither an end nor specific aims as such.

In addition, in Arendt's view a positive attribute of thinking is that it is entirely useless, "as useless, indeed, as the works of art it inspires,"[87] for thinking inspires the highest of human achievements such as poetry or conceptual art or other intellectual pursuits. The example of poetry (think of Schwitters's *Ursonate* or other useless examples of software art), in combining speech and action, demonstrates separation from the drudgery of instrumentalized human existence and a world driven by algorithms and instructions with predetermined outcomes. Furthermore, if more complex formulations of work are applied and the worker and tool combine as machinic assemblages, this comes close to Arendt's description of the tools becoming part of the laboring process in tune with the body, or replicating the body's movements and rhythms (her example being the deployment of labor-saving gadgets in the kitchen).[88] These machines draw labor and action ever closer together, not simply as labor-saving devices but as ways to recreate conditions. And yet since the time of her writing instrumentalism appears to have taken hold, and machines have become far too useful.

Reworking Arendt's distinctions in 2004, Virno thinks the separations of labor, action, and intellect have further dissolved. Whereas Arendt argued that politics imitated labor (as good action), Virno believes the opposite, that labor imitates politics—or indeed, that poiesis has taken on the appearance of praxis, as he puts it.[89] Since labor increasingly takes on the forms of action or indeed has served to depoliticize action, this explains the current "crisis of politics, the sense of scorn surrounding political praxis today, the disrepute into which action has fallen."[90] The problem lies in what Arendt already identified as the separations of making and action and knowing, and that one should not determine the other in a procedural means-end chain of events. Like Arendt, Virno cites Aristotle's famous passage from the *Nicomachean Ethics*: "For while making has an end other than itself, action cannot; for good action [understood both as ethical conduct and as political action] itself is its end."[91]

Reworking the same quote from Aristotle, Giorgio Agamben extends the understanding of action to gesture (referring to the distinction the Roman scholar Varro makes between *facere* and *agere*): "For production [poiesis] has an end other than itself, but action [praxis] does not; good action is itself an end."[92] The claim is that gesture not only disrupts the false distinction between means and ends but also occupies mediality itself, and in this way opens up the ethical dimension: "Politics is the sphere neither of an end in itself nor of means subordinated to an end; rather, it is the sphere of a pure mediality without end intended as the field of human action and of human thought."[93]

The ethical dimension is addressed by Virno through the idea of "virtuosity," a concept also derived from Aristotle who identifies two kinds of virtue, one intellectual and one ethical.[94] Ethical virtue for Aristotle is more than simply an intellectual decision on how to best act in a given situation, but also relies on ingrained habits of action negotiated through excess and deficiency, making virtue a disposition concerned with choice. Interestingly, Aristotle regards virtue as similar to musical skill, improved with practice. One who plays a musical instrument, not just playing something but playing it well, is like a virtuous human agent not just acting in the world but doing this well too. Both actions are learned by acting, as Aristotle explains: "The causes and means whereby every virtue is cultivated or destroyed are the same, just as in the case of all the arts. . . . If this were not the case there would be no need for teachers and everyone would be born good or bad. It is just like this with the virtues."[95]

To Arendt, similarly, certain activities demonstrate excellence in the public realm, constituted by the presence of peers and the formality that is required for a performance.[96] As an audience is required for the virtuoso performance, this also emphasizes the political sphere. Both politics and performances require a "publicly organized space," as does labor to be productive, as it involves communicative action.[97] Virno continues: "It is enough to say, for now, that contemporary production becomes 'virtuosic' (and thus political) precisely because it includes within itself linguistic experience as such."[98] Extending Arendt's definition of the public defined through speech, he links this to virtuosity, as a phenomenon that does not produce an end product independent of the act of speech itself, and that operates in public. The pressing issue for Virno is to ask: "What is the *score* which the virtuosos-workers perform? What is the script of their linguistic-communicative *performances*?"[99] The suggestion is that general intellect provides the "know-how on which social productivity relies,"[100] itself virtuosic in the sense that it combines technical skill, networked machines, and collective human intelligence. However, this should not have specific aims or an end in sight, as Arendt insisted too, but rather "virtuosity without a script, or rather, based on the premise of a script that coincides with pure and simple *dynamis*, with pure and simple potential."[101]

Performativity

Herein lies one of the challenges for those making program scripts that underscore various dynamic procedures of machines. As already established, a computer program undermines the distinction between its function as a score and the performance of the score, through its speechlike qualities. This is exemplified in the practice of live coding, where programmers make music in keeping with the expressive qualities of live performance, by coding in real time (using a command line interface, for example). To explain: "Live coding is where computer programming becomes performance art; improvising a performance using a programming language. This is made possible by the dynamic programming languages at the heart of all live coding environments. Sections of code are interpreted and added to a running program, so that a musician may enact thematic changes without a break in the sound. Thus the usual design-implement-test development cycle is discarded in favour of immediate actions and reactions more suited to creative exploration."[102]

Feedback.pl is a text editor written by Alex McLean with an unusual form of feedback. The programmer edits the code, which runs live while it is modified. However, the running code is also able to edit its own source code, so that the code is able to make fundamental self-modifications. Below is a simple example of some code modifying a comment, each time doubling up the letter "e" in the word "Feedback." That these self-modifications happen directly to the code being edited in real time puts the code visibly on the same level as the programmer. In a sense, the code embeds both action in-itself and action for-itself. Self-modifying code blatantly breaks the determinism of code and makes it explicitly performative. It demonstrates how programs operate together with the programmer, both relaying instructions and acting upon them in an uncertain relation.[103]

```
sub bang {
my $self = shift;

# Feedback
$self->code->[3]=~ s/e/ee/;
$self->modified;
}
sub bang {
my $self = shift;

# Feeeeeeedback
$self->code->[3]=~ s/e/ee/;
```

```
$self->modified;
}
sub bang {
my $self = shift;

# Feeeeeeeeeeeeeeeeeeeeeeeeeeedback
$self->code->[3] =~ s/e/ee/;
$self->modified;
}
```

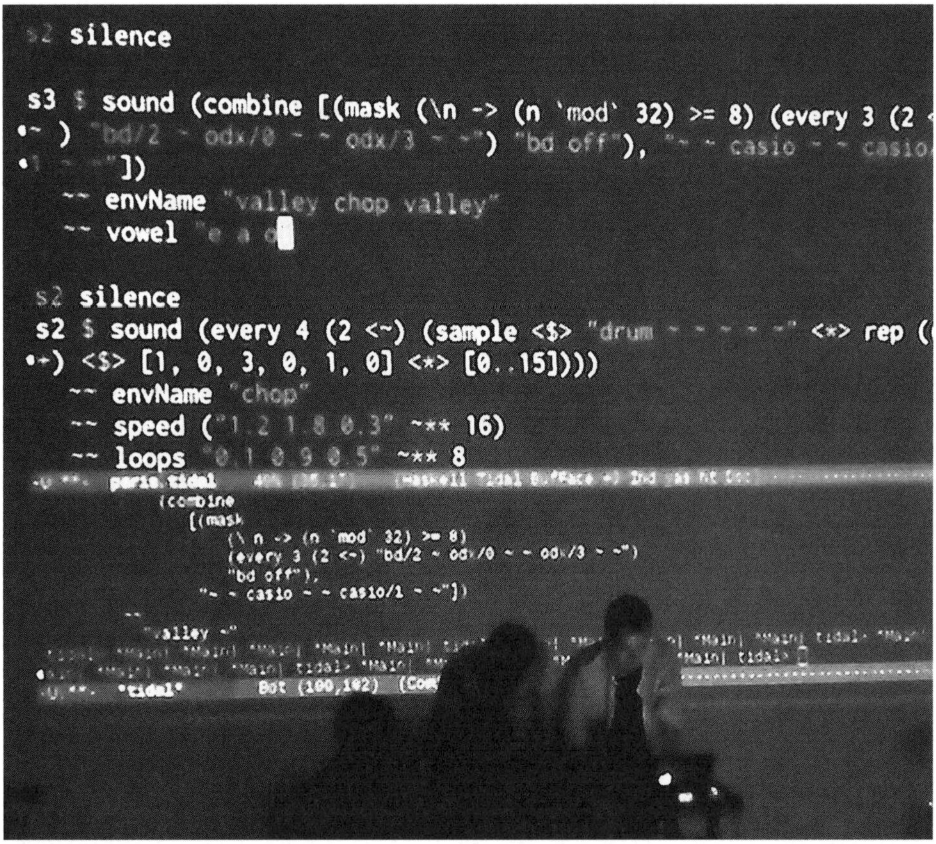

Figure 2.7
Live-coding performance by slub, at Maison Rouge, Paris, 30 August 2011. Image courtesy of slub.

It follows that many of the attributes associated with virtuosity could also be applied to the work of programmers, who demonstrate their technical and cultural agility through performances in public spaces. In this sense, the performativity of code breaks out of the means-end chain of following instructions to a predetermined end. The intervention of the programmer allows for an even more indeterminate approach and openness to other transformative possibilities, such as the possible and often unpredictable actions that result when a program runs, including the return of errors. The program performs the music with the programmer and vice versa, both relaying instructions and acting upon them.

In "Real DJs Code Live," McLean explains his approach to practice, emphasizing the active role of the programmer: "By describing a musical idea in code, we're describing it at a higher level than if we're entering notes into a sequencer. . . . I've tried sequencers and found it a slow, difficult, maddening way of doing music. There's an atmosphere of musicians being subservient to software. It really limits the kind of music that can be made. . . . Live coding places the human right back in the creative process so you can't really call it 'computer-generated' any more."[104]

The last part of the quote emphasizes the machinic and performative qualities and undermines the usual relations between coder and code for something far more dynamic. Similarly stressing the "performativity of code," Adrian Mackenzie clarifies that, "in terms of the contestations of agency associated with software, the primacy of coding can be seen as asserting the identity of programmers as the originators of software."[105] The agency of code workers may be often overlooked, but so too is a fuller description of the multiple processes and agents at work. In this way, the practice of live coding allows for an expanded sense in which plural aspects of coding work—writing, compiling, and running code—come to represent software as a whole.

Once software is defined as not only the program code but also the other materials required for the program to run, programmers become an integral part of the action. The act of coding becomes a prototype for action in broader terms, which includes a critique of the commercial imperative of software development and also the normative social relations associated with this. Like source code, these relations themselves become open to further modification, as is the case with the development of the Linux operating system. Mackenzie cites the Linux kernel (the core component of the GNU/Linux operating system), which he understands to have a particularly unstable relation to commodified software and hardware as the most pervasive example of free/open-source software development, by virtue of the file and process of the UNIX-like operating system and the enforcement of its GNU General Public License. He identifies the collaborative laboring process that underpins its efficiency: "The way in which the Linux kernel is produced and continually changed cannot be separated from its structure as a coding project. The performance of Linux as a contemporary operating system

Figure 2.8
radioqualia, *Free Radio Linux* (2001). Screenshot of homepage. Image courtesy of radioqualia.

cannot be detached from the circulation of Linux kernel code through code repositories and software distributions."[106] Its development is enacted through an ongoing collective and collaborative working process that Mackenzie considers to be a speech act. He refers to radioqualia's *Free Radio Linux* (2001), in which the source code of the Linux kernel was webcast over the Internet using a speech synthesizer to convert the 4,141,432 lines of code into speech (taking an estimated 593.89 days to read).[107]

The performance encapsulates the way that coding works in its fuller sense, as already described in relation to live-coding performances, and underpins the tensions around contemporary labor and coding practices. It produces an uncertain relation between the code object and code subject—the program and the programmers—and thus challenges property relations bound to the development and distribution of code. Like live coding, it is an example of machinic expression at the level of embodied communication or speech.

Referring both to live coding and to Virno's scores of virtuosos-workers, Simon Yuill further contextualizes coding practices through the example of the Scratch Orchestra of the late 1960s.[108] The historical parallel to improvisation serves to demonstrate how innovative forms of notation and performance techniques seek to free themselves from aesthetic and social conventions that are devised in relation to wider modes of production. Live coding can be seen to reflect present conditions, in which our lives seem to be increasingly determined by various scores and scripts but the possibility exists for more expansive conceptions of collective action, or more positive implementation of general intellect, and as indeterminate as one of the events itself with all its flaws and uncertainties of live performance.

Recomposition

If the economy is understood more and more in terms of scores and scripts, it is because new forms of labor are performative and linguistic. To demonstrate how work is now bound to speaking, Virno quotes Austin's *How to Do Things with Words*: "In the assertion 'I speak,' I *do* something by *saying* these words; moreover, I declare what it is that I do while I do it."[109] There is a biopolitical dimension to this, in the human capacity for speech and to make relations with others, based in what Virno calls "the faculty to speak; not work actually done but the generic capacity to produce."[110] Underlying this is the distinction that Arendt makes between the production process of work and labor that is more closely tied to life itself. The concept of general intellect is important to this too in emphasizing linguistic communication and social cooperation, enhanced by networks of machines and workers.

Christian Marazzi develops these ideas in *Capital and Language*, citing Austin as well to cast the powerful conventions of financial markets in terms of performative utterances, like "saying something makes that something true."[111] Marazzi cites Searle who refers to printed currency that is not simply a description of a fact but creates the fact; the "fact-that-one-speaks" produces the fact merely by the fact that it has been said. The recognition of the reliance of financial markets on collective speech acts underpins the viral operations of what Berardi calls "semiocapitalism" (he uses this term to signal the fusion of mind, language, and creativity).[112] This also establishes how the immaterial forces of language and money act on the soul in real terms, not at the level of metaphor, producing the fact of the present sickness of the economy.

According to Berardi, the soul has been broken and subjectivity made effectively soulless, as both desire and the soul have been colonized by capital and cast into depressed states.[113] He calls the situation in which the soul is put to work the "factory of unhappiness,"[114] and the control of happiness has become key to the health of the economy. The point is that unhappiness is encouraged to bolster productivity (as with so-called shopping therapy) but is carefully managed, for "the masters of the world do not want humanity to be happy, because a happy humanity would not let itself be caught up in productivity. . . . However, they try out useful techniques to make unhappiness moderate and tolerable, for postponing or preventing a suicidal explosion, for inducing consumption."[115]

Yet in the factories of unhappiness, things are beginning to spiral out of control, for example with the emergence of Facebook suicide groups such as the Facebook Mass Suicide Club or Hong Kong Facebook "suicide" group (sharing suicide methods and urging members to kill themselves on the same day in 2009).[116] Indeed, Berardi claims that "suicide is the decisive political act of our times," partly typified by 9/11 but more so by the example of the Finnish youngster Pekka Auvinen, who in 2007 turned up at school and shot eight people including himself, wearing a T-shirt with the sentence "Humanity is overrated."[117] What need to be rediscovered are forms of happiness tied to collective formations, such as the commons, and not to proprietary platforms like Facebook or Twitter (and more will be said on this in the following chapter, with examples of virtual suicides from these platforms). Alienation is accelerated as communication breaks down and subjects are left to babble, as in the case of *prozac.pl* cited in the introduction where "Hello world" is endlessly repeated.

The spread and speed of communications contributes to "psychopathology" according to Berardi, as collective intelligence is no longer able to adequately process the complexity of information being generated and we have forgotten the lyrics and rhythms that once bound communities together (as in the singing of folk songs). Happiness is exemplified by the public performance of songs. "For Marx, the privileged example of really free working—happiness itself—is 'composition,' the construction of the communist score . . . communism whose song will free the space in which it resonates, and spreads."[118]

A further example is Aaron Koblin and Daniel Massey's artwork *Bicycle Built for Two Thousand* (2009), using Amazon's Mechanical Turk crowdsourcing web service as mentioned earlier in the chapter. This time over two thousand recorded voices are collected and assembled into the song "Daisy Bell," the same song that was used in the first example of musical speech synthesis in 1962 (which made the IBM 7094 the first computer to sing a song).[119] Yet the comparison between the computer-synthesized vocals and the one created with distributed humans is not very encouraging, as both have been effectively synthesized. Despite payment (US$0.06), their voices like their souls appear to have been stolen at source. Interestingly, in Kubrick's *2001: A Space Odyssey*, HAL, the computer capable of reasoning, sings the "Daisy Bell" song as it descends into suicidal depression.[120]

The synthesized voice machine called the mobile phone is Berardi's example to demonstrate the network dependency and depressive tendencies that underpin contemporary production. With smart phones, voices operate as if in an echo chamber, for they have been effectively muted in the nullification of networked intelligence

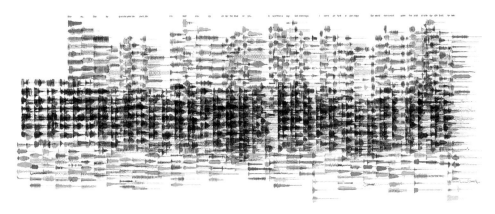

Figure 2.9
Aaron Koblin and Daniel Massey, *Bicycle Built for Two Thousand* (2009). Image courtesy of Aaron Koblin.

(replaced by so-called "smartness"). This is what Berardi means when he says that the soul has been put to work, such that information workers continue to work even when seemingly not working. Available for the iPhone, the parody game *iCapitalism* (2011) created by Crotch Zombie Productions provides an example in this connection, rejected from Apple's App Store for no good reason despite fulfilling their published criteria of acceptance.[121] The nature of the content was clearly the issue, despite the seemingly indiscriminate inclusion of endlessly trivial apps that are made widely available. The game is simple and ironic: the person who pays the most wins: "iCapitalism is the world's first game entirely driven by microtransactions. There is literally no gameplay outside of the ability to upgrade your character using real money."[122] It removes aspects of games like the amount of time required and skill involved, and without even the need for outsourcing development. As with all games, there are winners and losers, so in this case the platform owners win every time, but explicitly. Added interest lies in the fact that the time invested in the production of the app is wasted, as Apple developers invest their labor before its acceptance in the marketplace.

The speech act in this case is aggressively locked down, underlining how subjectivity in the form of the voice is somehow captured and fragmented in the use of these telecommunications devices. The digital network more generally facilitates the spatial and temporal globalization and precaritization of labor, but it is the "cellular" qualities of this that recombine semiotic fragments endlessly to produce semiocapitalism, according to Berardi.[123] The most important commodity of late capitalism, the mobile phone, is the instrument through which this takes place, melting our brains both literally and metaphorically through its use of microwave radio frequencies.

But all is not lost. Berardi reads the present financial crisis as a precondition for the return of the soul, like the return of the repressed. If neoliberalism attempted to capture the very essence of life, it will always ultimately fail, as it wrongly assumes "that the soul can be reduced to mere rationality."[124] The soul is even more unpredictable than the mind or body. It is something far more unknown and complex, its potentialities irreducible to the market or even language. It is something closer to poetry or the voice,[125] and to the indeterminate code acts that have been described thus far that demonstrate the potential for the recomposition of collective action, using improvised scripts and esoteric programs.

3 Coding Publics

There has been much recent interest in revisiting Arendt's ideas, in particular in relation to a reconceptualization of publicness.[1] As outlined in the previous chapter, Arendt identifies the centrality of action to politics, as distinct from other activities related to work and labor, because action is necessarily linked to plurality, to performative actions in public. Although all human activities are conditioned by society,[2] only action and its relation to politics are entirely dependent upon a "paradoxical plurality of unique beings," who with actions and speech introduce themselves to the world.[3] In Virno's work, further recognizing the communicative dimension of capitalism, the reference to Arendt is emphasized because of what he considers the relative ineffectiveness of political action today.[4]

Yet the human capacity to act in the world is enduring, even under the most difficult circumstances according to Arendt, a view underpinned by her support of grassroots political movements at her time of writing (such as the citizen councils that arose during the Hungarian Revolution of 1956). It is interesting to note that at the time of writing now (summer and autumn of 2011), the enduring power of social movements and public action has been proved again, as witnessed by the various "pro-democracy" campaigns in North Africa and the Near East (so-called "Arab Spring"), movements opposing state budget cuts to the public sector, protests against the marketization of education, and the political agenda around Internet freedom and the controversies surrounding WikiLeaks.[5] An example of the latter is the recent "denial of service" attacks by the loosely organized group of "hacktivists" called Anonymous.[6] Emerging from the online message forum 4chan,[7] the group coordinated various distributed denial of service (DDoS) attacks using forums and social media websites, where instructions were disseminated on how to download attack software to bombard websites with data to try to throw them offline, and target sites were publicized such as the organizations that had cut ties with WikiLeaks (such as MasterCard, Visa, and PayPal, through "operation payback"). Their slogan reflects their constitution as a public: "We are Anonymous. We are Legion."[8] Most recently (since 17 September 2011), the Occupy Wall

Street movement, with its rapid spread to other parts of the world, also seems apposite in its reappropriation of common space in places where financial power is centered (squatting its symbolic sites, to express indignation about the handling of the financial crisis since 2008).[9] Adopting the "#Occupy" hashtag,[10] the wider Occupy movement is described in terms that embody publicness in a wayward culture of financial calculation and social inequality: "We are the 99%."[11] Perhaps it can be claimed that the concept of publicness has itself been occupied in these recent events.

Both examples serve to underscore Arendt's view that the political realm necessarily arises out of acting together, as a plurality of unique individuals, in "the sharing of words and deeds."[12] It is collective activity that relies on the infinite capacity to speak freely and act in public, and this is what constitutes publicness in her terms. But what does it mean to speak and act now, at a point when production processes have taken on these forms, when scripts and scores seem to predetermine the actions that are executed? The understanding of action is rather different from in Aristotle's time, when to act outside of the commons was considered "idiotic" (derived from the term *idion*, indicating life spent in the privacy of one's own).[13] The public realm, a realm of equals, was distinguished from the inequality of the private household (although those not considered equal, such as women and slaves, were not able to enter public life). Notwithstanding the clear inequalities of the public sphere today, the fundamental contradiction is revealed in the idea of public interaction from the privacy of an online platform or home computer as an attack on networked intelligence. F.A.T.'s parody of the Occupy movement, *Occupy the Internet!* (2011), resonates with this problem, suggesting revolution from the comfort of your home computer.[14] By pasting the following JavaScript into an HTML file, an "animated GIF army" appears on the webpage:

```
<script src="http://occupyinter.net/embed.js"></script>
```

It may be possible to "force-occupy" the global investment banking and securities firm website Goldmansachs.com in this way, and even contribute animations and "pithy words," though this is surely not significant in terms of political effect.[15] Yet even with the apparent triviality of this project, other possibilities are registered that might encourage wider interpretations of what constitutes public action, and prompt the writing of alternative scripts. *Protest* (2011), one of Pall Thayer's microcodes, hints at this possibility.[16]

```
#!/usr/bin/perl
sub protest{
        reset $wall_street;
        return our $future;
```

```
}
until($equality){
        protest;
}
```

These examples of current activity aside, the concern of this chapter is to consider more mainstream implementations of software released into the public realm, to register the conditions under which this is done, and to examine the consequences in terms of "coding publics." Exaggerated claims for the inherent publicness of the Internet or for its reinvigoration of the public sphere, as well as the ways that scale-free networks like the Internet naturalize the fantasy of global unity, foreclose wider discussions of the underlying command and control structures. Participatory and collective forms of communication and political expression may become part of the very mechanism of guaranteeing their nullification—in the production of empty speech acts.

If the reliance on proprietary logic seems to legislate against a plurality of voices with unique attributes—the unavoidable contradiction in the case of most social media—then to voice opinions points to the limitations of the organizational models on offer and the freedoms they claim to augment. To speak or voice opinions in this way is rendered fundamentally paradoxical. In the use of the term "voice," it should be clarified that a double sense of representation is invoked: both voice that relates to sound like speech, and voice that stands for expressions of political opinion in representational democracies. Perceived misrepresentation of voice has been recently opposed using the tactic of "mic check" (sometimes called "people mic") to amplify public opinion. Through call and response, protesters drown out (or occupy) the amplified voice of authority.[17]

In *Why Voice Matters*, Nick Couldry's concern is to foreground a politics of the voice that recognizes the capacity for social cooperation rooted in the human condition, echoing Arendt's position. Our voices represent a material precondition, through the acquisition of language and other processes of ideological recognition but also through embodiment, rooted in the relation between voice and action (as indicated in the two previous chapters). The reference to Arendt confirms the importance of this issue, how actions combined with speech partly constitute us as political subjects and in this way express forms of agency, hence the dangers of the colonization of speech by proprietary technologies. The relationship to politics is crucial for the argument, yet it is consoling to recognize that voices operate both within and beyond politics.[18] Here lies a crucial point, that despite all attempts to capture our voices in simulations and telephonic extensions, the issue of excess confirms how voices remain resistant to their encapsulation as they oscillate between private and public domains.

Public domain

Drawing on an understanding of networks, the chapter examines first some of the sociotechnical conditions that underpin public forms, especially given the contemporary importance of networked communications in constituting the public domain. It is not that the idea of publicness is not used, of course, especially in the discourse around social media, but that it is heavily compromised in its application. The proliferation of privatized social networking and current developments in service-based platforms (what has become known as "cloud computing") provide pertinent examples of such compromises, and carry profound consequences in relation to the commodification of networked intelligence introduced in the previous chapter. To reiterate the problem with reference to Virno, what is at stake is that the publicness of the intellect is not a positive public force unless it is at the same time political. He is warning against the dangers of what Arendt identified as "publicness without a public sphere," which seems to have become so painfully prevalent under current conditions.[19] What seems to be lacking in discussions of the public domain is a deeper way into the concept of the public itself.

Unless this dimension is developed, the human capacity to speak and act in the world remains mute, exemplified by the fantasy of enacting a revolution from the comfort of your home computer. Despite wild claims in the popular press for Twitter's or Facebook's central role in sweeping aside authoritarian regimes in 2011, the supposed new tools for protest and solidarity represent contradictory forms of publicness (inasmuch as they rely on privately owned platforms). In "The Revolution Will Not Be Tweeted," Jon B. Alterman explores the exaggerated claims with some important qualifying details.[20] Although social media clearly played a part in the uprisings, he points to the continued role of old media like television, which wasn't considered "sexy" enough to be widely acknowledged in the press; and furthermore that there have been "revolutions" at all is contestable, given that existing political structures largely remain intact despite the departure of specific leaders. Nonetheless it is interesting to note how the use of social media has allowed for people to identify themselves more readily as "activists," simply through their ability to create and share content. Therefore, and if Twitter has become the media of choice for political mobilization, what does this indicate about politics and its popularization? It is sobering to consider, as a parallel case, Simon Cowell's reported partnership between Twitter and his *X Factor* TV show, to enable the world to tweet its response to the various "artists" vying for celebrity status on the show.[21] The lack of hierarchy of value here should not be surprising, as "what Cowell understands is that there is no expropriation afoot here at all. There is no vulgarization, no cheapening, no hierarchy of value on Twitter or anywhere else in the socialsphere."[22] The cultural relativism is part of the issue, in situations where pluralities are largely homogenized and our actions made ever more productive for communicative capitalism, whether in the realm of crass entertainment or political protest.

Purification

Responding to paradoxes of this kind, the Museum of Ordure is a "self-institution" that has a special interest in the management of human waste and its impact on the concept of the public sphere and civil society.[23] Its early policies on preservation included running a server-based script that accelerated the process of decay of its digital objects, resulting in unpredictable and often sudden glitches appearing in the images and captions that constituted its public collection.[24]

Since the identification of "ordure" (such as rubbish, waste, anything unclean, or shit)[25] indicates value judgment, issues related to the social web have further inspired the development of the museum's website, in taking the detritus of communications and cataloguing it as empty speech acts. A dynamic collection of images and captions is currently produced with feeds from sites like 4chan, mixing diverse contents (from popular trivia such as images of cats to news reports on contemporary protest movements); its Twitter feed @museumofordure, although since suspended, used the hashtag #ordure and retweeted various others (like #revolution and #insurrection).[26] Using techniques similar to other cultural institutions' addressing the issue of public engagement, the museum's aim is to reveal the excess of capitalist production.[27] Its core purpose is further explained, in the About section of the website.[28]

Inspiration also derives from Dominique Laporte's *History of Shit* (first published in French in 1978), which verified modern power to be founded on the aesthetics of the public sphere and in the agency of its citizen-subjects, but that these are conditions of the management of human waste. Laporte insists that in parallel to the cleansing of the streets of Paris from shit, the French language was similarly cleansed of Latin words to establish official French without "foreign leanings" (according to an edict of 1539). Both public space and language were purified in parallel, as purification requires submission to the law: "If language is beautiful, it must be because a master bathes it—a master who cleans shit holes, sweeps offal, and expurgates city and speech to confer upon them order and beauty."[29] Thus he contends that language was purged of its "lingering stink" to become purer, and that sovereign power is confirmed through purified speech: "There the muddied voices and their dialects are expurgated of their dross, losing their pitiful 'remnants of earth' and the vile fruits of their dirty commerce." Thus language "cleanses the fruit of their common labor, elevating it to the divine place of power freed from odor."[30] The desire for clean language as well as clean streets sublimates shit and demonstrates an expression of new biopolitical forms of control over the body and subjectivity, one where the market is now sovereign (rather than the state or indeed king or queen). Can we say the same of code, and

HOME
The Museum of Ordure

About
• Mission
• Partners
• People

Explore
• Past projects
• Current projects
• Future projects

Collection

Research
• #ordure
• Resources

Blog

Support

Terms of Service

The Museum of Ordure explores the cultural value of ordure through its projects and ongoing public collections.

About

The Museum of Ordure is a speculation on the roles and dichotomies of the museum where the contradictions of the civilising processes are in the context of the real politique. Its aim is to reveal an underbelly where the collective unconscious breaks out into the world. It follows the traditions of exposure from the middle ages through to the present day. Naturally enough it is itself an element of the conditions it examines.

Beginning with the most basic human endeavours we come quickly to the point of excrement; as all that which is regularly voided from the body. Survival is dependent on the ingestion of material sustenance, food, (although there are claims that it is possible to live on air), and its intimately connected discharge of waste materials. Shit has been relegated, and tabooed. Since Thomas Crapper's commercial exploitation of the invention of the water closet in the nineteenth century we deposit stools into water which are then immediately flushed away. We hardly glimpse at or have any contact with what we produce, and are conditioned to regard it as extraneous and noxious. It tends to smell offensively because the management of the human body is often perfunctory and casual. This in itself is a subject for consideration. To what extent is the body knowingly polluted? And why? Is the body polluted also by fetishised engagements with mental and physical hygiene? Can the "body politic" ever be anything other than a polluted body? Is art a form of pollution?

Ordure is an ever present shadow signifying to all that is deemed unworthy. Unwanted, discarded debris induces choking urbanisations, smearing land and urban scapes alike. It thrives in the sway of the brutalising exploitation of natural materials and processes usually dealt with elsewhere, (where labour markets are cheap). The interchange is filled with abrasions, natural disasters, and human sacrifices. The world as a rubbish dump. Aesthetics profits from such profligacy.

Recently acquired
for the collection

FYI, JP Morgan Chase donated $4.6 million to the New York City... 2011

BROWSE THE COLLECTION »

The Museum of Ordure
South Studio, Walker House, 6-8 Boundary Street, London E2 7JE, UK

MUSEUMofORDURE   ABOUT   EXPLORE   COLLECTION   CONTACTS

Figure 3.1
Museum of Ordure's homepage (2011). Image courtesy of Museum of Ordure.

that pervasive technologies such as mobile devices that are to be found on the streets are similarly cleansed?

Developments in cloud computing seem to provide similar examples of purified forms. Software and network services merge into one platform, through which people access the Internet using their mobile devices and shiny tablet computers. This sense of purification is exemplified by the Apple paradigm of software development with specially conceived proprietary "apps" (for iPhones and iPads) that close off users from the underlying impurities ("stink") of code, through the clean interface of the App Store and iTunes for instance. These current developments are crucial for a fuller understanding of the suppression of political expression in the public realm, and the ways in which public intellect is becoming ever more privatized (the example from the previous chapter, of the rejection of *iCapitalism*, is a case in point).

This builds on what the valorization process already sublimates in production, which Marx identified plainly in the *Grundrisse*: "In fact, of course, this 'productive' worker cares as much about this crappy shit he has to make as does the capitalist himself who employs him, and who also couldn't give a damn for the junk."[31] In the social factories that produce the contemporary junk of telecommunications not much has changed, and the workers who build the devices are "treated inhumanely, like machines."[32] As well as the human costs, the environmental consequences of over-production are there for all to witness, as more and more environmental pollutants are dumped around the world as a consequence of an ever-expanding demand for telecommunications gadgetry.[33] Like the tradition of examining feces to determine the health of the organism, the health of the economy can be judged by the way it manages its waste.[34] Can the value of communications using a platform like Twitter be determined in similar terms?

Speech theory reminds us that meanings of words are not derived merely from their logical structure but from their public usage (just as Laporte clarifies, in quoting Barthes, that it is not the word *shit* that smells).[35] There can be no such thing as a private language. Is it not the same with computer languages and platforms more generally, that they begin public and that it takes perverse effort to make them private? The case for collective working is further expressed by the inherent structures of technologies that encourage sharing and self-organization at all scales of operation, rather like the plurality at the heart of the human condition, as already stressed in the work of Arendt. Moreover, it takes ideological effort to privatize, in historical parallel to the turning of common land into private property in the enclosure movement in England at the end of the eighteenth century, or indeed in the more recent example of patenting of gene sequences and stem cells as part of the so-called "second enclosure movement."[36] These examples stand as violations of the commons and inherent publicness that are part of the human condition (coming close to what Hardt and Negri have referred to as "common-wealth").[37]

Ownership

Western societies have tended to stress a view of ownership tied to individuality, but this should be considered a perversion. Much of the anthropological work around sharing and gift cultures helps to substantiate this claim, to be discussed in more detail later in the chapter. At the heart of the problem is a set of assumptions about sharing and producing in terms of the generation of cultural and economic value. As James Leach points out, under capitalism creative ideas are extracted from the commons and modified, such that the issue of ownership and property arises as a problem bound to individualism rather than the public domain. In other parts of the world, especially historically, ownership related to creative work in a far more pluralistic manner, connected to quite different spiritual and ideological principles.[38] Leach gives the example of "spirit songs" in Papua New Guinea, which, although based on ancestral heritage, are constantly changed and modified but with the underlying condition that "spirits and people belong to one another."[39] In such a model, ownership is bound to relations between people and spirits, and as multiple agents for future modification (like the singing of folk songs that belong to the people/folk). Leach explains how this is distinct from the conventions of copyright based on the production of commodities: "People do own images, and ideational forms, but these are not owned in objects. In other words, they do not rely on the separation of mental/ideational creativity from its instantiation in an object that can then be owned as property."[40] As collective speech acts, the songs are generated by collective voices, and, in keeping with oral traditions, the voice remains somewhat resistant to its commodification.

In the case of songs, the process of production is privileged over product. Leach's argument is that comparisons can be drawn with the principles of multiple ownership expressed in software development, in which the conditions for creativity are not necessarily bound to individualized private property and the products are immaterial. A contemporary example is the development of the GNU/Linux operating system, where each individual's work is valued in the context of the multiple efforts of all contributors, although the relations are still expressed between people and things with copyleft/GNU GPL.[41] Even enlightened public domain licenses, as noted in chapter 2, are paradoxically locked into legal frameworks that treat ideas as objects rather than processes. To Leach, this necessitates a critique of current ideas on valorization that disregard a deeper understanding of creative processes and commons-based production.[42]

Commons-based peer production is one model of collective creation in this respect, challenging traditional descriptions of productive activities and standard organizational forms that turn social relations into proprietary objects. There is indeed heady speculation on the social implications of peer production and the way it poses problems for traditional understandings of organizational structures and the productive activities of publics. Information technologies may have made some of these processes pervasive and more efficient, but these are hardly new ideas, as historians and anthropologists reveal. In Yochai Benkler's pragmatic view, peer production works because it best matches human capital to projects and the public realm is good for innovation.[43]

The Foundation for P2P Alternatives also investigates some of the changing business models and the challenges to definitions of social wealth: "a distinction between revenue and benefit sharing that the commons is founded upon (on the one hand, extracting monetary value from social processes and on the other imagining more sustainable alternatives to capitalist economy that have collective benefit)."[44] Its founder, Michel Bauwens, optimistically thinks, "A peer to peer system in this respect might be considered 'post-capitalist' in the production of a social relation based on sharing and the common good."[45] He argues for a better understanding not simply of revenue sharing but of benefit sharing through peer production and commons-created platforms, and recognizes the antagonisms between the different social contracts of Creative Commons and the GNU General Public License, as well as the different business models these suggest. He concludes that the GPL is superior as it allows for commercial use and free exchange, or what he calls "non-reciprocal logic."[46] But is it not the case that the ideals of peer production and the commons are turned into objects and hence expropriated by legal frameworks? Perhaps Virno's phrase, the "communism of capital,"[47] better expresses the paradoxes of implementation in the way that the commons is made to follow proprietary logic rather than reject it altogether in "commonism" (in the sense that it infers communism), as part of an ongoing process of seeking collective autonomy.

Freedoms

Further exploring such contradictory forces, Christopher M. Kelty's *Two Bits: The Cultural Significance of Free Software* explains two interlocking narratives of software development.[48] One is the story of free software, reaching back to the 1980s when software freedom was promoted in resistance to proprietary software; the other is that of open-source software emanating from the dotcom boom and free-market thinking that free software offers economic benefit (as Benkler remarked). Releasing source code therefore represents a number of ambiguities relating to freedom, both a belief in open standards and yet also a cynical business move to capitalize on sharing and free labor. The detail is useful, as the two intersecting terms are often simply conflated into "FLOSS" (free libre open-source software) and confounded by a far too straightforward description of producing and releasing software, rather than a wider discussion of the competing ideologies they espouse. According to Kelty, to put it simply free software describes a social movement, whereas open-source is a development methodology.[49]

To the Free Software Foundation, it is also necessary to clarify the concept of "free": "'Free software' is a matter of liberty, not price. To understand the concept, you should

think of 'free' as in 'free speech', not as in free beer."[50] In other words, and as Bauwens
also explained, "free" does not mean noncommercial, and there is no contradiction
between selling copies and offering them gratis. The history of this line of thinking
is impossible to chart; it relates to the human condition, as old as the sharing of
stories or songs (or "just as the sharing of recipes is as old as cooking," as Stallman
puts it).[51] He asserts that a program can be described as free if the users have certain
freedoms protected by copyleft conditions to ensure that conditions associated with
freedom are maintained in further use, and access to source code is clearly a precondition for this.[52]

In making the connection to freedom of speech at all, Stallman is building on an
ethics that emerged from programmers and hacker communities beginning in the
early 1990s, such as early USENET communities, and notably with the widely circu-
lated paper "Freedom of Speech in Software" (1991) by the programmer Peter Salin,
arguing computer programs to be literary (like Knuth in *The Art of Computer Programming*) and therefore unfit for patents, although appropriate for copyrights and, thus,
free-speech protections.[53] Yet the analogy to freedom of speech provides numerous
ambiguities in relation to its guarantee under international law through numerous
human rights instruments. According to Article 19 of the Universal Declaration of
Human Rights, "Everyone has the right to freedom of opinion and expression; this
right includes freedom to hold opinions without interference and to seek, receive and
impart information and ideas through any media and regardless of frontiers."[54] Article
10 of the European Convention on Human Rights similarly provides the right to
freedom of expression, but like Article 19 is also subject to certain restrictions that are
"necessary in a democratic society."[55] This allows restrictions for the interests of
national security, or public order, or protection of public health and morals, and so
on. Speakers' Corner in London exemplifies the paradoxes of a "free democracy" in
this way, as anyone can speak on any subject but only on condition that the police
consider the speeches to be lawful, and despite the fact that free speech is prohibited
in most other public spaces in the UK.[56] How can people speak meaningfully in a situation where the rights to free speech are enshrined in hypocrisy? Similarly, free speech
on the Internet is subject to both state and market regulation, and further compromised by the increasing use of filtering software and surveillance practices.[57] The case
of WikiLeaks has recently stressed the multiple contradictions around these issues
too.[58]

Underpinning the discussions of free and open-source software expression at a more
fundamental level is the sharing of source code, itself rooted in the history of the
UNIX operating system and its pervasiveness. If UNIX became the most widely used
and portable operating system, it was also always caught between the competing forces
of the public domain and private interests. Again, Kelty examines the history of this
development in more detail as well as the adoption of the TCP/IP protocol for network

capability. He explains how it was the need for interoperability and networking that led to the adoption of an open-systems method in the 1980s, as technical systems diversified. Openness became the working paradigm at this time, on account of its roots in cybernetics and its relation to post-Second World War economics and the trend toward the opening of markets, in what became the free-market project of neo-liberalism.[59] Crucial to an understanding of this ideological aspect is that the antonym of open is not "closed" in this case but "proprietary," as Kelty points out, demonstrating its significance to ownership regimes and the expanding global marketplace.

In "The Contestation of Code," David M. Berry also points out how openness has tended to be understood through definitions of transparency and freedom that are based on individualistic notions of how society might be better organized.[60] He thinks the arguments tend to be rooted in an "engineering philosophy of technology" at the expense of its wider cultural and ethical significance.[61] In this sense, the Free Software Foundation operates rather too much like a craft guild for programmers,[62] with a radical project in terms of technology but one not fully formed into a coherent political position. In Berry's view, the issues related to the ways that labor and property are encoded into software tend to be overlooked, and as a consequence an understanding of freedom and control is somewhat occluded by code, making access to its source in production all the more necessary. The practice of coding requires a broader context in order to better recognize its active part in the constitution of public networks, in which it operates more like a performing artist than a software engineer perhaps. Further drawing on Arendt's work on speech and action, and also on an understanding of code as a speech act (acknowledged in a footnote), Berry suggests that the free software movement offers the potential for political action based on a "politics of the commons."[63] The commons becomes a crucial term in this respect, particularly in relation to intellectual property issues, and almost interchangeable with the idea of the public domain or public sphere.[64]

Public networking

To echo the words of Virno, the practice of coding is of little use if it remains outside the public domain, for this is where politics resides. At issue is a better understanding of what constitutes a social formation or body politic, the ways in which political power is contingent upon networks, and the ways that objects operate within those networks. Part of the difficulty simply lies in the fuzziness of the terms in popular usage.[65]

Drawing on Werner Heisenberg's uncertainty principle,[66] Bruno Latour tries to productively develop key concepts that open up the performative dimension of the social, such as the nature of group formations, actions by multiple agents, and objects that demonstrate agency. Taken together, this is what he describes as the "actor-network," which does not have a single source of action but acts in plural ways as the coming together of complex, diverse, and interlinking agencies locked into uncertain social relations. Heisenberg's principle states that the very act of measuring certain physical properties disturbs the thing being measured, and hence makes the measurement unreliable. By way of analogy, Latour explains that on a theatrical stage it is never clear who is acting (as the actor is part of a larger apparatus of acting), and it is unclear what is authentic and what is not.

This is exemplified in a networked performance by Christophe Bruno called *Human Browser* (2005), in which a human actor, using wireless headphones, hears a text-to-speech audio that comes directly from Google search results in real time, and simply speaks the words (thus somewhat embodying the software).[67] The human speaker, the software, and the network together combine into a paradoxical plurality of agents that constitute a satire on agency and freedom of speech.

It is uncertain who or what is executing the action or speech, like a puppeteer who does not have absolute control over the puppet,[68] once again evoking Benjamin's allegorical description of the chess-playing automaton and its winning combination. In such ways, multiple agents become network actors, producing machinic assemblages that reflect the sociotechnical performances of networks more generally. What

Figure 3.2
Christophe Bruno, *Human Browser* (2005). Image courtesy of Christophe Bruno.

is missing is a fuller understanding of the ways that humans, objects, and networks express power relations in these assemblages, and whether this might constitute a public of sorts.

Inequities

There has been a tendency to think of networks as equitable systems, but it has been well established that certain connections are granted greater privileges than others. Networks are often viewed as inherently random, simply because their operations appear too complex to comprehend; but randomness remains a misleading description, as "relative connectedness" is articulated through the density of connections in scale-free networks.

Albert-László Barabási uses the mathematical concept of the "power law" to explain how complex networks demonstrate "directedness," in other words how they are organized preferentially.[69] The Italian economist Vilfredo Pareto observed that 80 percent of peas were produced by 20 percent of pea pods;[70] and many other phenomena seem to fall into similar inverse relationships (as in the popular adage that 80 percent of wealth is owned by 20 percent of the population). Although this 80/20 rule (an example of a power law) seems rather imprecise, it does offer some scientific insight into the politics of self-organization. That the "rich get richer" is not random, of course, but a highly selective process, demonstrating what Barabási calls "preferential attachment," which in turn generates a free-scale network and a conception of "fitness."[71] Like fitness, relative weakness, even in natural systems, is supported by interconnectivity to the system as a whole. In a similar way, "cascading failures" evince the interconnectedness of elements when a local failure redistributes responsibilities to linked nodes, as when the collapse of the US mortgage market in 2008 had a ripple effect around the world. The rich got too rich, and the fitness of financial markets turned out to be a weakness after all.

The historical development of the Internet is a further example of the way that any one node in a network is compensated by the interlinking connections to the system as a whole. This informs the logic of its development, of course, funded by the Defense Advanced Research Projects Agency (DARPA) of the United States Department of Defense to provide a robust communications infrastructure able to withstand local failures.[72] Its mechanism of command and control was expressed through distributed networks that would supersede centralized or decentralized ones, as these were considered far too vulnerable. The adoption of packet-switching networks, which informed the development of Arpanet, came to characterize the Internet as well.[73] The idea was to break messages into units (like a cut-up poem) and then route each message unit along a functioning path to its ultimate destination, where it would be reassembled to form a coherent message once more. But once again the focus on technical development alone, at the expense of wider cultural and ethical considerations, leaves little room for a wider conception of agency that, if considered embedded in object-subjects under dynamic network conditions (as Latour thinks), is evident in all aspects of the network. The question of who is pulling the strings continues to be pertinent.

The oversight is something that Alex Galloway has also identified in his attention to the concept "protocol" (such as TCP/IP, or transmission control protocol/Internet protocol), referring to the "recommendations and rules that outline specific technical standards."[74] Protocol is developed as more than simply a metaphor for power, although clearly a useful one all the same, and indicates *correct* behavior within pro-tological systems more broadly. In a similar way to the contingency already outlined, computers in networks agree technical standards of action such that the protocols "govern" usage at the level of code.[75]

Control

The governance issue is important as various protocols connect machines to each other, and when it comes to the Internet they are also subject to the DNS (domain name system) information stored in databases, with a relatively small number of root servers. In the current model, it is important to note that the Internet's address struc-ture (DNS), which enables communication between the world's computers, is managed by the not-for-profit Internet Corporation for Assigned Names and Numbers (ICANN) under contract to the US Department of Commerce.[76]

This is not to say that control is necessarily a problem, of course; but a problem exists in that standards are set according to certain ruling interests. Therefore this becomes a political issue; in the example of social media platforms, there are many examples of political groups having their Facebook or Twitter profiles disabled. Con-sequently, according to Ned Rossiter, there is an urgent need for new institutional forms that reflect relational processes, to challenge the existing incompatibility of hierarchical and centralizing systems of governance.[77] What he refers to as "networked organizations" stand in contrast to emergent "organized networks," which are more horizontal, collaborative, and distributed in character. The latter hold potential to transform social relations, and this is demonstrated in coding practices and the devel-opment of technical platforms for social exchange. As ever, it is the way the social relations are organized that makes this a political issue.

A project that aims to make these sociotechnical relations somewhat apparent is Rui Guerra/INTK's *www_hack* (first developed in 2008), a JavaScript installed on a host webpage that allows all visitors to that page to observe each other's virtual presence through their mouse movements.[78] The script contacts a server where all the individual mouse positions are stored, and then displays them in real time so that the user is made aware of other users and encouraged to reflect upon the internal architecture of the web and its centralized server-client paradigm. The script is installed simply by including the following line of code on the header of your webpage:

```
<script language="javascript"
src="http://www_hack.v2.nl/www_hack_me_please.js"> </script>
```

It is designed to reveal inherent power structures, in contrast to decentralized forms (although admittedly JavaScript is proprietary, indeed owned by Google, so there is an underlying paradox all the same).[79] What becomes clear is that the experience of the web is bound to inherent paradoxes that are reflected in its technical organization.

This point is also clarified by Rossiter, who stresses that organized networks represent relative autonomy but only if they engage both horizontal and vertical modes of interaction. He explains: "The tendency to describe networks in terms of horizontality results in the occlusion of the 'political', which consists of antagonisms that underpin sociality. It is technically and socially incorrect to assume that hierarchical and centralizing architectures and practices are absent from network cultures."[80] It is not enough to argue for distributed forms alone, that is, without at the same time understanding that this is also a structure of power. He is invoking Carl Schmitt's notion of enmity (in *The Concept of the Political*, 1927): "The political is the most intense and extreme antagonism, and every concrete antagonism becomes that much more political the closer it approaches the most extreme point, that of the friend-enemy grouping."[81] Moreover, Schmitt's critique of liberalism, and of consensus-based models like representational democracy, lies in the recognition that antagonism is an inevitable component of human societies. Referring to Arendt once more, politics is defined in the contradictions at the heart of action: between acting and being acted upon.[82] There is no avoiding this antagonistic relation.

If modern democracies are characterized by fake consensus, then representation and any assumptions about a settled totality of active citizens are revealed to be an expression of publicness without a public sphere. Indeed many commentators have drawn on Schmitt's insistence on the recognition of antagonism, but with rather different conclusions than his legitimation of authoritarianism. For instance, Rossiter sees this as an opportunity to develop better organization from below, and rethink ideas of democracy uncoupled from sovereignty. Citing Virno's *A Grammar of the Multitude*, he explains: "While networks in many ways are regulated indirectly by the sovereign interests of the State, they are also not reducible to institutional apparatuses of the State. And this is what makes possible the creation of new institutional forms as expressions of non-representational democracy."[83]

Nevertheless, and as already established, the plurality of nodes in networks does not guarantee a more inherently democratic order; indeed, it arguably serves to obscure its authoritarian substructure. This represents one of the problems of the free software movement too, that although it stresses important community-driven processes and action, it tends to avoid the wider discussion of vertical structures of power, and hence politics more broadly. More plainly, it can be seen how the organizational structures of social media underplay antagonism in favor of friendship and thereby occlude the political dimension, inferring Schmitt once more. The publicity for the mythologized film narrative of Facebook's development, *The Social Network* (2010), reveals the sublimation of enmity: "You don't get to 500 million friends without making a few enemies."[84]

The command and control structures of the social networks operate in such ways. This is what Galloway and Eugene Thacker refer to as the "network-network symmetry" of power, to support their claim that networks and sovereignty are not incompatible.[85] Indeed, they claim that "sovereignty-in-networks" is "exceptional," thus making a further reference to Schmitt, who established the contiguity between sovereignty and the "state of exception." Taken up by Benjamin too, this indicates the legal system's "monopoly on violence," and the paradoxical way that violence is seen to be inadmissible and yet in exceptional circumstances is seen to be necessary, such as when security issues are at stake.[86] Further developed by Agamben,[87] the claim is that the state of exception, although initially described as a provisional measure in exceptional circumstances, has become the working paradigm of modern government. Under this logic, state power uses preemptive violence against an identifiable enemy so that its use of power appears legitimate, or is deemed necessary, despite the active contradiction with its own legal and moral frameworks. The duplicity is evident in the way those deemed to be a danger to national security can be taken into custody and detained in ways that erase their individual human rights, turning them into what Agamben calls "noncitizens."[88]

If the sovereignty-in-networks is exceptional too, it is also demonstrated in online platforms that offer the promise of democracy yet in practice are only served through centralized ownership and control. For instance, the social web mediates social relations in this manner, offering the freedom to communicate but through the exception that relates to both state and market principles, in parallel to what has already been said about the conditional aspects of freedom of expression more generally. Facebook regularly shares information with government agencies and purges activist's accounts, such as those of campaigners trying to organize antiausterity protests in 2011, including the UK Uncut and Occupy movements.[89] A closer look at the terms of service of these platforms confirms ways that ownership is carefully managed, parodied by a consumer advocacy blog with the suggestion for new terms: "We can do anything we want with your content. Forever."[90] Users are happily granted access to the means of production but not ownership. The underlying contradiction is clear: "The social web facilitates an unprecedented level of social sharing, but it does so mostly through the vehicle of proprietary platforms."[91] In such ways, freedom is extracted by a service to serve the free market, not free expression.

In terms of the market, the exception is that platforms take what is given for free and monetize it. To take Facebook as an easy target again, content is produced for free, and its "value" is extracted from users by platform owners. Value is produced in ways that reflect the capture of affect under the conditions of informational capitalism and the so-called "attention economy."[92] But it should be emphasized that Facebook is a financial venture with an effective business plan, and perhaps the financial aspect has been underplayed in the discussions that tend to focus on attention rather than the political economy. The statistics demonstrate the point: US$355 million generated from the sale of "audience commodities" in 2010, and US$2 billion in financial rent through investments in 2011.[93] To Bauwens, this suggests a business problem: if users create social wealth and the platform owners monetize it, what kind of return can be created for users, and how might the benefits be shared more openly?[94] In practice, there appears to be a more pragmatic tradeoff between ethical principles and use value, with users signing away rights to private platform owners in exchange for public sharing services, often in full knowledge of the compromises this involves, and therefore without producing alienation in the traditional sense.

This pragmatic analysis may provide new insights into emergent economic models that have developed new techniques for value creation, but these are clearly also new techniques of control and exploitation, in what appears to be the growing financialization of the human condition. These techniques are all the more effective as they involve the user's willing subjectivity in the process, as Lazzarato explains: "The production of subjectivity ceases to be only an instrument of social control (for the reproduction of mercantile relationships) and becomes directly productive, because the goal of our postindustrial society is to construct the consumer/communicator— and to construct it as 'active'."[95] Value is created and extracted in this way, bound to free labor power and the willing actions of citizens and organized through the insidious techniques of "soft control."[96] Control is not exerted externally by force, but instead exploits the already emergent behavior in the system. The self-organization of individual agents in the network seems to give them freedom to act, but in reality local exceptional rules are present that compromise their actions. Therefore, if what is captured in the process is the ability to act freely in public space, what Arendt referred to as a paradoxical plurality of unique beings, then how to act? How to rupture the relations between acting and being acted upon, or between programming and being programmed?

Exits

Reflecting the fashion for seeking autonomy from these processes of value extraction, as well as from command and control protocols, a number of critical artist projects have emerged that demonstrate various tactics of refusal, from the now familiar DDoS attacks to other exit strategies in the case of social media.

One such case is moddr_'s *Web2.0 Suicide Machine* (2009), an example of "unfriending" from Facebook, MySpace, Twitter, and LinkedIn. Its website publicity explains:

Figure 3.3
moddr_, *Web2.0 Suicide Machine* (2009). Image courtesy of moddr_.

"Liberate your newbie friends with a Web2.0 suicide! This machine lets you delete all your energy sucking social-networking profiles, kill your fake virtual friends, and completely do away with your Web2.0 alterego."[97] The program is performative: it logs in to the user's account, changes the profile picture into a pink noose, and changes the password (in case you are tempted to resurrect your profile), then proceeds to delete all friends, one by one. moddr_ claimed it was protecting the right to commit assisted virtual suicide, something Facebook disagreed with, citing the way the machine collects log-in credentials and scrapes their pages, all violations of their terms of service. But their objection demonstrates their duplicity, as it is well established now that Facebook holds on to personal information for their own shadowy purposes even after deletion of accounts. The example indicates the enduring importance of privacy issues, as well as the issue of control that underpins network operations.

A contemporaneous example is the Facebook hack by Les Liens Invisibles, *Seppukoo* (2009), also a platform for committing virtual suicide in an overtly ritualized manner.[98] Making the conceptual references clear, the project title refers to the Japanese ritual suicide of *seppuku* (literally "stomach-cutting") and the stubborn refusal to fall into the hands of the enemy even at the cost of one's life, following the samurai code of honor. Furthermore, the project is inspired by *Seppuku!*, the ritual suicide that some members of the Luther Blissett Project committed in 1999 to declare the end of their

Figure 3.4
Les Liens Invisibles, *Seppukoo* (2009), detail. Image courtesy of Les Liens Invisibles.

multiple identities project (and the death of net.art as a temporary autonomous zone).[99] Such projects seek autonomy from the deadening forces of proprietary platforms, and the enemy is identified as part of a process of asserting the political dimension of networks (reflecting the need to identify the enemy in the development of early computer tracking systems or first-person shooter games).

The similarities between the projects are clear, but Les Liens Invisibles further explain the important principle of encouraging a shift from individual to collective action through the use of viral dissemination, and thus "deactivation might potentially represent a denial of this supervalorization of one's virtual body, hence put into action what the Tiqqun group calls a human strike."[100] It should come as no surprise that Facebook was fast to challenge this intervention too, issuing a cease-and-desist letter claiming that the work infringed their rights in accessing information for services furnished by third parties. The *Seppukoo* About page explains the double standards: "Suicide is a free choice and a kind of self-assertiveness. Unfortunately, Facebook doesn't give to its users this faculty at all, and your account will be only deactivated." Like Mephistopheles, Facebook holds on to the user's soul once the terms have been agreed.

To cite another paradoxical gesture, Paolo Cirio and Alessandro Ludovico's *Face to Facebook* (2011) attempted to liberate people's profiles by stealing one million of them from Facebook, effectively stealing back what has already been stolen in the first place.[101] The profiles were then used to form a fake dating website, lovely-faces.com, to reveal the levels of exploitation of personal details, and the inextricable link between circuits of affect and profitability.[102] Both the dating site and Facebook share the empty promise of friendship and love, and with different purpose in mind reflect how language and affect have become increasingly economized. As social attention is captured, one of the terrifying effects of the attention economy is first to commodify social relations and then to sell them back in compromised form.

In *Democracy and Other Neoliberal Fantasies*, Jodi Dean explains this in terms of the construction of willing subjectivities: "Communicative capitalism captures our political interventions, formatting them as contributions to its circuits of affect and entertainment—*we feel political, involved, like contributors who really matter.*"[103] This leads her to conclude that participatory democracy is not the answer to contemporary political problems but a *symptom*. Active participation remains a fantasy in her terms, like clicking a button on an online petition for instance. This is something that Les Liens Invisibles have taken quite literally in another project, their online petition platform *Repetitionr* (2010).[104]

In contrast to petition platforms such as iPetitions,[105] the *Repetitionr* platform provides an online petition service for campaigns where success is guaranteed, as just one click is all it takes to generate up to a million automatic fake signatures. It uses the

Figure 3.5
Les Liens Invisibles, *Repetitionr.com* (2010), homepage. Image courtesy of Les Liens Invisibles.

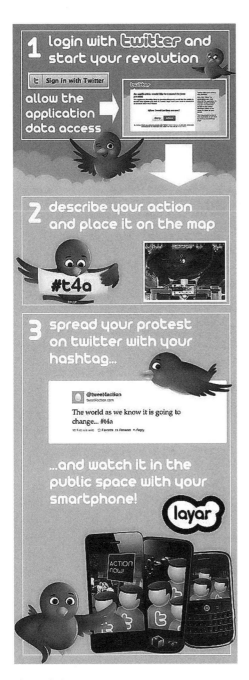

Figure 3.6
Les Liens Invisibles, *Tweet4Action* (2011), detail of "How it works?" Image courtesy of Les Liens Invisibles.

Figure 3.7
UBERMORGEN.com, *[V]ote Auction* (2000–2006). Image courtesy of Fabio Paris, Brescia, [DAM], Berlin, Carroll/Fletcher, London.

tactic of "overidentification," in which a position is pushed to its extreme, to question the effectiveness of online activism.[106] In their related project, *Tweet4Action.com* (2011), they further respond to the exaggerated claims of social media to influence political processes, and use Twitter and a Smart Phone augmented-reality application called Layar to create "Twitter revolutions" from the comfort of your armchair.[107] The project was developed and released against the backdrop of "pro-democracy" protests in North Africa and the Near East to draw attention to associated hypocrisy.

It would appear that consumer capitalism and democracy have become interchangeable in representative democracies, as made explicit by UBERMORGEN.com's media hack *[V]ote Auction* (2000–2006), an online service allowing consumers to directly participate in the US electoral process by selling their votes to the highest bidder.[108] Temporary injunctions followed from US courts for alleged illegal vote trading, and the server was shut down without notice.[109] The inconsistencies around this inspired another project, a public shutdown service called *The Injunction Generator* (2003), consisting of software to autogenerate an injunction which is then sent to the DNS registrar, to the site owner, and to the media.[110] In this way, the public is encouraged to take the law into their own hands, and is able to send a cease-and-desist letter to force a site to take its contents offline. The legal systems that legitimate the hypocrisies of governments are appropriated and finally democratized.

As can be understood from these examples, the human subject is no longer defined as an active citizen but as a consumer, reacting to the rationality of the market rather than the limits of government.[111] Further drawing on Michel Foucault's lectures on "governmentality," it can be argued that neoliberalism (as distinct from liberalism) has replaced the regulatory function of the state and its relation to the market with the market itself.[112] The goal of government becomes to persuade the public to take an active role in its own subjugation, and to generate certain types of subjectivity in line with the participatory logic of markets. This is an important foundation for a critique of social media and the ways in which the energies of peer production and social exchange have been expropriated from the public by the market. In this sense, the generic marketing term "Web 2.0" is just another example of capital recuperating the democratic potential of "new" technology for the privatization of public assets. It *sells the public its own publicness*—as with the paradox of selling off a publicly owned company and persuading the public that they can then buy shares in it, or public taxation subsidizing the financial failures of banks.

There are numerous examples of platforms that extract value from peer production, but thankfully there are also others that try to hold on to such value, reinforcing Marazzi's connection between financial markets and collective speech acts (such as experiments with P2P currencies, for instance).[113] The current attacks on public welfare services as part of so-called austerity measures seem to press the point of producing alternatives, as public education and the welfare system are eroded by the reductive logic of financial capitalism. The problem is to identify when speech acts are ventriloquized ones.

Public for-itself

It is no longer a question of who speaks, as it seems that everyone is encouraged to babble with limited registers and effects, tweeting incessantly their every thought and calling everyone a friend, however superficially they may be known. To press the point, the script *import_friends.py* below attempts to make friends with all the members of the social networking site Twitter. Once given access to a Twitter account, it "follows" all of its Twitter friends, and all their friends, and so on. In this way it

operates in a similar way to *Samy*, a viral "worm" that in 2005 brought its author Sam
Kamkar over a million MySpace friends in less than one day, as well as soon after a
conviction for felony.[114]

```
#!/usr/bin/env python
import twitter

api = twitter.Api(consumer_key='xx', consumer_secret='xx',
                  access_token_key='xx', access_token_secret='xx')

def befriend_friends_of(friend):
    for fof in api.GetFriends(friend.GetScreenName()):
        isFriend = filter(lambda f: f.GetScreenName()
                          == fof.GetScreenName(),
                        friends)
        if len(isFriend) == 0:
            api.CreateFriendship(fof.GetScreenName())
            friends.append(fof)
            # this function calls itself, creating a
            # recursive explosion of spurious friendships
            befriend_friends_of(fof)

friends = api.GetFriends()
for friend in friends:
    befriend_friends_of(friend)
```

If the concept of the public has lost some of its efficacy and its actions have
been largely nullified, it is because the rationality of the market as an organizing
force tends to offer choices, experiences, and subjectivities that suit its narrow definitions. If neoliberalism is largely a "voice-denying rationality," as Couldry thinks,
it is because of its domination by economics: "Voice is undermined by rationalities
which take no account of voice and by practices that exclude voice or forms of
its expression."[115] Yet it does not really seem to be the case that certain voices are
suppressed or silenced, but that they are emptied of significant meanings. Voices
are ever more present but cleansed and purified, and even dismembered from
the body.

Recombination

Privatized technologies clearly play a vital role in distancing speech from affect in a
situation where action and words have lost their power, to echo Arendt's point. To
Berardi, the fundamental struggle remains between machines for liberating desire and
mechanisms of control over the imaginary, and clearly this can be applied to speech
and coding cultures. Like some of the examples introduced in the last section, he
suggests processes of "dynamic recombination," such as the refusal of work, the inven-

tion of temporary autonomous zones, and free software initiatives, as potential ways out of the conundrum.[116]

In "Code Is Speech," Gabriella Coleman cites examples of programmers engaging deeply in political protest against the dominant regime of intellectual property and defending their sense of autonomy over production, enforcing their "rival liberal legal regime intimately connecting source code to speech."[117] After all that has been said to this point about the claims of the free software movement, perhaps its political position becomes more coherent when considered in line with Arendt's stress on the relation of collective action to politics. If the liberatory claims for free software seem exaggerated at times (or rather too enclosed), this is partly due to the ways the argumentation is bound to the problematic discourse around free speech rather than action, or than the relations between the two. In its rejection of proprietary code, the free software movement can be understood as an example of emergent and self-organizing public action, what Kelty identifies as a "recursive public,"[118] extending Arendt's definition of a public through speech and action to incorporate technical and legal infrastructures. Thus publicness is constituted not simply by speaking, writing, arguing, and protesting but also through modification of the domain or platform through which these practices are enacted, making both technology and the law unstable. In this way, Kelty draws attention to the limitations of our received understanding of the public, explaining that a recursive public is "vitally concerned with the material and practical maintenance and modification of the technical, legal, practical, and conceptual means of its own existence as a public; it is a collective independent of other forms of constituted power and is capable of speaking to existing forms of power through the production of actually existing alternatives."[119]

The argument is that free software is a special kind of speech act, able to modify the discourses and infrastructures through which it operates. As a consequence, a reconceptualization of political action is required that takes into account traditional forms of expression, such as freedom of speech, with freedom as it relates to coding cultures, encapsulated by the phrase "running code" to describe the relationship between what Kelty calls "argument-by-technology and argument-by-talk."[120] But if speaking, acting, and running code have become somewhat incorporated into the mechanisms of domination, especially in the case of service-based platforms where there is no code left to share, then the publics associated with coding need to resist market logic with a broader set of political alliances. Furthermore, the pluralities of voices and actions can only be effective if this paradoxical sense of totality is understood, for this is where politics resides.

Reciprocity

It is fundamentally paradoxical for a group to speak or act with one voice (*vox populi*, the voice of the people). Making the distinction between thoughts, words, and actions,

Etienne Balibar maintains that it is impossible to act with one voice, for no one can be forced to think like another or speak like another.[121] Individuals give up their right to act freely on this basis, but not necessarily their right to think freely. He explains how the liberal tradition has tended to emphasize the distinction between individual opinions and collective actions, and between private and public realms, whereas to Balibar they "reciprocally 'underwrite' each other."[122] In other words, tendencies toward authoritarianism and democracy operate not in opposition but in reciprocal relation. He is drawing upon Spinoza's *Tractatus Theologico-Politicus* (published in 1670), which describes the relation between state and individual citizen, holding that a strong reaction will be provoked if there is an attempt to suppress freedom of speech. So it follows in the liberal tradition that a mechanism is developed that allows people to imagine their voice is heard on an individual basis and as part of the collective, and this actually helps to strengthen the state itself, even when the voices are critical. Following this understanding, the state opens up the widest possible domains for the expression of opinions that become constituent of its own power, and even protesters no longer act as "an obstacle to the sovereign's power (*potestas*), but as an active, constitutive element of the power (*potentia*) of the State."[123] The process is recursive, based on "reciprocal limitation" (or "self-limitation") in which each element "interiorises the utility of the other."[124]

According to Spinoza, democracy rests on this ability of citizens to determine their fate through the actions of the collective sovereign, in exchange for the ability "to construct a common will and to determine their common good."[125] In this way they become collective individuals, a paradoxical formulation that comes close to Arendt's description of a plurality of unique individuals. Yet the myth of equality continues to underwrite the logic of liberal democracies, with the idea that somehow the diversity of our voices can be accounted for through the ventriloquism of the representational process where individual voices are homogenized as one. This is how Spinoza addresses the paradox: "The collective is an 'individual of individuals' with a body and a soul (the body politic)."[126] The reference to the soul, which Berardi adopts from Spinoza too, represents the way that the collective-individual operates through imagination and reason, both through desire and effective rule.

Individuals must be enabled to voice their diverse opinions, both for and against the dominance, in order to legitimate it. Sovereignty is in effect enforced through the totality of the diverse opinions and is not in conflict with the operations of plural networks, as previously stated. If this is the case, and networked sovereignty operates through reciprocal relations, then we also need to critically review the oppositions that are perpetuated between free software initiatives and web platforms, between peer-to-peer networks and server-client architectures, as well as between public and private ownership regimes. These examples also demonstrate how sovereignty has been transferred to the market and its hold over telecommunications networks as a new authoritarian voice of democracy. The market seemingly allows for diverse consumer choices and rights, in exchange for a strengthening of its own power and expanding consumption of technological devices that purport to allow for freedom of expression. In other words, the voices that the system allows strengthen the force of the market and its very hold over the voice.

This is also what Couldry seems to conclude when he asks: "What if, under particular conditions (themselves connected to Neoliberalism), the general space for 'voice' that mainstream media provides works in important respects to amplify or at least normalize values and mechanisms important to Neoliberalism and, by a separate movement, to embed such values and mechanisms ever more deeply within contemporary cultures of governance?"[127] To those who have read Balibar, the question is rendered rhetorical.

Autonomy

Given what has been said of the effectiveness of alternatives and reciprocal relations, how can the increased privatization of digital networks and public services be resisted? What has been suggested so far is that a deeper engagement is required with the concept of voice, its relation to networked intelligence, and running code, to point to some possible strategies. To reject the amplified voice of authority and refuse its command is to refuse the economization of language and expression. For Groys, like Arendt, politics operates largely with language, and the critical task is to refuse this subordination so that human action can become relatively free (like software). Otherwise, "every protest is fundamentally senseless, for in capitalism language itself functions as a commodity, that is to say, it is inherently mute."[128] The public speaks freely and remains mute in reciprocal relation.

The identification of paradox is critical to this understanding. Groys refers to Plato's views on the power of language, and in turn to Socrates to stress the defining role of logic which itself relies on paradox. Groys explains the importance of Socrates in going beyond smooth speech (of the Sophists, who specialized in the use of rhetoric for teaching excellence, or virtue): "It emerges that such speech only superficially appears to be well-knit and coherent. In its internal structure, however, it is obscure and dark because it is paradoxical."[129] Furthermore, the smooth speeches of the Sophists were made for financial reward; their speech acts were commodities for those who could afford them. So speech is evidently not pure, nor free, however rhetorical, but inherently paradoxical, and this confusion continues to the present day with code too. Evidently, "no one who speaks under the condition of freedom of opinion knows what he actually means. Although most people believe that their ideas contradict other ideas, and are polemically directed against other ideas, these ideas in fact contradict only themselves. Every speaker says what he intends to mean, but he also says the opposite of this. All opinions that circulate in the free market of ideas are characterized equally by this state of internal contradiction, internal paradox."[130]

Does this hold for software too? The rules of logic, expressed today through the operations of software, attempt to obscure this paradox through proprietary forms, but this always fails ultimately as program code is paradoxical too. Indeed, it is an extreme case, and like speech is tied back to itself even when attempting to explain something entirely outside of itself. It is recursive, and its incompleteness or insufficient totality is what drives the possibility of transformation. In Hegelian fashion, Kelty describes the free software movement in these terms, as it transforms from a "class-in-itself to a class-for-itself" and therefore represents radical transformation through self-recognition of the conditions of its publicness.[131] For it to do this, and to act politically, an epistemological understanding of recursivity is important, to explain how the public comes to know something and at the same time incorporates the subject position of the knower with the thing known. In other words, the public knows it is incomplete, and its lack of totality informs the ways in which it can reinvent itself as a body politic, and eventually become a public for-itself.

The public function of the intellect is crucial here, and this leads Berardi to trace Hegel's move from in-itself to for-itself further, via Marx's adaptation, to the concept of "mass intellectuality."[132] The interlinking references assert the line of argument that the publicness of the intellect is not a positive public force unless it is at the same time recognized as political. According to Berardi, only the autonomy of intellectual labor from economic rule can save us from the forces of capitalism, and he is invoking collective and networked intelligence. The speculation in the present book is that coding practices offer a means to recombine speech, action, and intellect in this way.

Can we imagine autonomous coding practices that generate possibilities for actually existing alternatives; or a coding public that is also able to recursively act for-itself? This would represent an expression of networked intelligence that has separated itself from proprietary forces with some degree of autonomy from economic determination, rediscovering the actuality of what it means to speak and act freely in public. The example below that closes this chapter, *export_friends.py*, destroys each of your Twitter friendships in turn, so you are left following no one at all. Just before the process of unfriending, however, the program sends a message, asking each friend to meet one of your other friends in the same public space. In this way, the social network that relates to the proprietary space of Twitter is replaced with an embodied social network. The new social network graph formed by these messages is "directed," in that friend X is invited to meet friend Y, but friend Y is not invited to meet X but a different friend. As they all are instructed to occupy the same place at the same time, these invitations will generate unexpected encounters. The gesture aims to indicate something of the enduring capacity of the public to modify preprogrammed scripts that appear to limit their actions and render their actions and speeches otherwise void. It also serves to open up some of the conditions for transformation in the face of over-powering forces that wish to shut down and deny access to the source code of alternative possibilities.

```python
#!/usr/bin/env python
import twitter, random

api = twitter.Api(consumer_key='xx', consumer_secret='xx',
                  access_token_key='xx', access_token_secret='xx')

friends = api.GetFriends()
for friend in friends:
    friendName = friend.GetScreenName()
    friend2 = random.choice(friends).GetScreenName()
    message = "%s wants to meet in the main public square tomorrow" %
(friend2,)
    api.PostDirectMessage(friendName, message)
    api.DestroyFriendship(friendName)
```

4   Code for-Itself

To Arendt, whatever can be known or experienced can only make sense in relation to speech and action, and to the human capacity for thought and thoughtlessness. In making the distinction between contemplation (*vita contemplativa*) and action (*vita activa*), she concludes that it is not possible to go through life without acting in it, whereas contemplation is optional. Her proposal is simple, "it is nothing more than to think what we are doing."[1] She distrusts science as a context in which "speech has lost its power," where a language of mathematical symbols has replicated spoken statements but cannot be translated back to speech.[2] These are the conditions in which thoughtlessness seems to have gained ground, and technology is rendering us ever more thoughtless.

Berardi's understanding of the problem is rather similar to Arendt's in his observation that we have been acquiring language from machines, not from other humans (namely, from our mothers), in situations where the learning of language and affectivity have been largely separated.[3] The problem of language acquisition is extended to intellectual and social behavior, and he calls this a catastrophe of modern humanism, in which we no longer have sufficient attention spans for love, tenderness, and compassion. We are more and more estranged from affect as speech becomes commodified, and is increasingly rendered using devices locked into neoliberal markets that have no interest in the voice as a sign of human solidarity.

Things are rather differently described in early coding cultures. In Hayles's *My Mother Was a Computer*, she charts how in the 1930s and 1940s, people, mostly women, were employed to do calculations and were referred to *as* computers (Hayles appropriates her title from a chapter in *Technologies of the Gendered Body* by Anne Balsamo, whose mother was one of these computers).[4] Kittler's *Discourse Networks* also refers to how the mother's voice haunts reading, making reference to the period around 1800 when children were taught using phonetics, to sound out and voice words. By 1900, he observes that distinctions were drawn between noise and signal.[5] This further detail helps to explain Berardi's lament on the conditions for the teaching of speech and the disconnection from the body, and importantly serves to stress how the voice of the computer connects the construction of particular kinds of subjectivity and learn-ing practices that use informational systems. It might be said that what is lacking is closer attention to nurture and the articulation of human feeling that cannot be expressed by words alone.

If the voice also haunts computing in this way, it interpellates us in new ways that affect our thinking processes, intellectual capacities, and abilities to express empathy with others. It is these kinds of interactions of code and language that also interest Hayles, as artificial languages proliferate and in recognition of the acknowledged cul-tural influence of human languages on constructions of subjectivity. Her concern is that programming languages are too easily dismissed as artificial and of lesser conse-quence.[6] In technologically advanced cultures, language and program code interact all the time in complex ways, and even mothers and computers can become confused in their assigned normative functions. Central to this approach is that the understand-ing of code (as of speech and writing) is constituted ideologically (through what Hayles calls a "worldview"). Like speech, program code is active in the world and has a lived body, indeed is intimately connected to a social body. The issue that has occupied the book thus far is about control of that body, its expurgation, and related processes of autonomy activated through coding practices.

Execution

The human capacity to speak and act is enduring, as Arendt has stated, even when language itself is used as an apparatus of power against it. This is partly because lan-guage is paradoxical, and holds an innate ability to transform itself as well as those who are constituted through it. The relation between speech and action has been explored in previous chapters: to speak is to actualize something, announcing the intention to produce an action in the moment of doing so. It is also clear that language has effects, as it acts for us and against us, and this is what Butler has referred to as "linguistic vulnerability," confirming the unerring power of language to affect us from our beginnings, as with the case of the Althusserian call to order as a form of violence on the human subject.[7] Butler's point is that violence is embodied in language, not simply in the way it might be used to incite a violent action or in the ways that lan-guage reflects social domination more generally, but in the way that it produces meaning. This relates to Hegel's observation that there is something inherently violent in the capacity of language to represent a thing, what he calls "its essencing ability," which is equivalent to its symbolic death. As it stands in for something, "it dismembers the thing, destroying its organic unity," and forces the thing into a field of meaning that is outside of itself.[8]

This also happens with source code and perhaps in a more extreme manner, as code exceeds natural language through its protocological address to humans and machines.

It says something and does something at the same time—it symbolizes and enacts the violence on the thing: moreover, it *executes* it. In addition to these symbolic and physical forms of violence, there is also something that comes close to "pure violence" (in the sense of Benjamin's essay "Critique of Violence" of 1921), action that is directed not to other human beings but to the symbolic powers and operating systems that reign over them.[9] Pure violence appears to come from nowhere, as "an expression of pure drive, of the undeadness, the excess of life, which strikes the 'bare life' regulated by law."[10] One might speculate that code might similarly express pure means through collective actions like DDoS attacks, SQL code injection techniques,[11] the spread of viruses, directed at the sovereign technical infrastructures that already exert forms of violence on clients through the enforcement of restrictive terms of service and the like.[12] The hacktivist tactics of Anonymous, mentioned in the previous chapter, or of LulzSec, the splinter group who have been "Laughing at your security since 2011!," exemplify such ways of thinking.[13]

When Virno confirms how language radicalizes "aggression beyond measure,"[14] he is drawing on Aristotle's description of contingency at the heart of our use of language. Besides the enduring capacity to speak and act, his interest is in the ability of the human species to execute "innovative actions" that he likens to recursive plays of language.[15] Underpinning political possibilities, for Virno, is the simple fact that the human animal is capable of modifying its forms of life, of innovating new forms.[16] This is what enables and produces innovative action, in the sense that newly invented forms might diverge from established rules and perceived or consolidated norms (based on Chomsky's idea of innate creativity previously discussed, although Virno prefers not to use the term creativity, as it has become so instrumentalized through the creative economy agenda). He cites the example of jokes, as demonstrations of the ways that "linguistic animals give evidence of an unexpected derivation from their normal praxis."[17] Rather than taking jokes to be Freudian clues to the workings of the unconscious, he regards them as examples of sociolinguistic games that demonstrate innovative techniques and possibilities for transformation. He explains that this happens in two main ways: first, by demonstrating how divergences in following rules often result in changing the rule itself; and second, through the incorrect use of semantic ambiguity.[18] Of course his point is not the content of the jokes, which might of course be political (and yet perhaps counterproductive in serving to obscure or normalize the issue), but the linguistic apparatus or the "*logicolinguistic resources* that jokes utilize."[19] He characterizes this sense of linguistic innovation as "how to do new things with words" (after Austin once more), in which doing something relies on public action and also "presupposes and revives a public space," thus reiterating earlier references to linguistic-communicative performances that necessitate a public space.[20] So, to Virno, innovative utterances are similar to collective speech acts where speech constitutes action in and of itself, as potential speech in-itself.

The argument relies on the recognition that innovative action uses linguistic and performative resources in similar ways to jokes, and is thus able to intervene in the workings of contemporary capitalism because language has been absorbed at a structural level into the political economy. Behind the possibility of innovative action is the enduring ability of language to create unexpected relations between multiple speakers, as speech is necessarily shared and collective. Language constitutes what Virno calls a "pure institution" (before and beyond the law), as it underwrites all other institutions, and emphasizes that the human animal is ready-made for language but only enters into language through socialization.[21] To Virno, this confirms the biopolitical dimension of the human animal in the world, and the ability to act in unexpected and innovative ways to challenge institutional norms and presuppositions of normative logic. Moreover, if the subject is to some extent constituted in language, then to think that someone saying and doing something is a straightforward demonstration of agency misses the point that actions are always already encoded, like the innate ability to produce sounds from the body, however abstract they may seem. The historical subject is always ready to speak and act, whether conscious or not yet conscious of the need to do this. It is in recognition of this fact that the public is always able to act for-itself as a body politic, however constrained the conditions may appear to be.

Negation

When Virno describes "not-yet public forms of government,"[22] he is pointing to the ways in which the public is always ready for collective action in this sense. They are able to construct innovative forms of self-organization by negating received organizational forms, similar to the way a recursive public is able to modify the means through which it is constituted as a public (discussed in the previous chapter). To Virno, this possibility of reinvention is explained through the interplay of innovation and negation inherent to language. In contrast to representational democracy, for instance, he refers to *non*representational forms inspired by a nondialectical understanding of negation. Like negative feedback, a determinate negation becomes a constructive influence on the system as a whole, allowing it to self-regulate.[23]

To clarify the concept of negation a little more, the distinction needs to be made between mere difference (something is not something else) and the more fundamental claim that something is not something else but depends on it to exist. This is the basis of dialectical logic, where the role of negation, and its further negation (negation of negation), become important for understanding some of the ways in which dominant ideas attempt to reproduce themselves, even when an oppositional stance is taken. This is why it has to "die twice," as Žižek puts it (in tarrying with the negative), in order to reject its symbolic confines.[24] But this is not quite what is meant by Virno, who recognizes that neoliberalism is a negative condition that requires further negation, not through negative dialectics but on the basis that negation is embedded in the paradoxes of language. For him, it is the determining role of language that needs negating to protect the possibility of a reciprocal *non*recognition: "the implicit presupposition of rhetorical persuasion and, in general, of the permanence of a public sphere."[25] His reading of the system of language reveals its inherent paradox in the way it represents, as it both does negation (by identifying what something is not) and is negation (inasmuch as it can only signify something): "The negation, or something that language *does*, is understood, above all, as something that language *is*."[26]

The concept of negation appears to operate like a speech act too, countering the authoritative call to order and opening up alternative possibilities outside the "sovereign autonomy of speech."[27] Moreover, Virno speculates on forms of politics that recognize the ways that sovereign forces try to restrain these inherent capacities for innovation or social transformation, as with the illusion of free speech as a mechanism of power. This leads him to conclude that self-government needs to adapt itself directly to the "linguistic aspect of the human species."[28] Therefore it becomes necessary to produce paradoxes between the determinism of grammatical rules and the ways in which speech is always to some extent out of control (something Butler previously identified). This is in recognition that the linguistic-communicative aspects of capitalism have become central to its structural logic, as well as its potential reinvention. If both negation and innovation are constituted in language, like human subjectivity, then any sense of agency afforded to it is also constrained and activated in reciprocal relation.

The contingency at the heart of this is explained neatly by Žižek, who describes the illusion of free choice through the notion of interpellation and how it chooses its subjects. He refers to the "vulgar liberal notion" of freedom of choice as a "fundamental choice by means of which I 'choose myself'."[29] *Forced choice*, on the other hand, is explained as the subject freely choosing the inevitable, such as the historical subject's recognition of class consciousness (class in-itself). The subject recognizes itself as encoded, "always-ready" for action, and only in this way can begin to act freely. The subject is thereby called by history to act in the way it should act and take the right course of action. In Žižek's explanation and in parallel to the perceived determining role of language, this is not ideological manipulation at all as it is already programmed in advance and there is simply no choice to be made. This holds for speech, as it preexists itself; it is speech before speech, or speech in-itself. Things are decided before they are enacted and they act on us, not the other way around. But if this is the case, Žižek asks, are we simply turned into computers or thinking machines,[30] or input-output machines as Laporte suggests? Is it that human subjects are preprogrammed and merely execute their preprogrammed instructions and scripts?

If human action is largely rendered ineffective under current conditions, perhaps this is because language has become instrumentalized by machine logic, and thereby disconnected from human feelings. Virno concludes: "For political anticapitalist and antistate action there is no positive presupposition to be vindicated. Its eminent duty is to experiment with new and more effective ways of negating negation, of placing 'not' in front of 'not human'."[31] Should we not do the same with the figure of the programmer and with programming in general, remove it from the determining conditions of the market that strip it of human fallibility and the possibility of innovative action? Like freedom of choice, is it only possible to begin to think of free software as a result of the self-consciousness of conditions in recognition of it being programmed in the first place? If so, then there really is no real choice at all and all software can be considered to be free at source. Code is always ready to execute, in the move from in-itself to for-itself, and it seems verified that information wants to be free.[32] Code can express freedom only inasmuch as it is able to execute the right course of action.

Coda

By indicating that language is taught by computers and not by another caring human, Berardi points to the way that human expression and social attention have become overtly economicized (as part of the so-called "attention economy").[33] Like fast speech, he thinks interpretation has become schizophrenic, and that the relations between metaphors and things, representation and life, have become thoroughly confused, leading to the conclusion that "a hyper-stimulation of attention reduces the ability to critically and sequentially interpret the speech of the other who tries and yet fails to be understood."[34] The inability to produce collective speech acts leads to tragic consequences in terms of the human psyche, according to Berardi, as of course language acts on the construction of subjectivity itself. This separation of language from affect leads to a situation in which this excess of signs, obsessive accumulation, and accelerated communications leave little time for love, tenderness, and compassion, or even for contemplation, as Arendt lamented.

If we no longer have sufficient attention spans for free thinking or love, then perhaps we simply haven't recognized that both have been there all along. Again an example from Žižek, quoting Bertrand Russell, helps to clarify the point: "I did not know I loved you till I heard myself telling you so. . . ."[35] In other words, love preexists the knowledge of it. A similar paradox underlay Berardi's reading of the source code of the "I Love You" virus (which spread through communities of the Internet in 2000).[36] Although seemingly declaring love, the message "love letter for you" if opened erased documents from your hard drive and then propagated itself by sending new copies of itself through the address book of your mail program.[37] Berardi effectively negates the negation by turning it into spoken poetry.

In another example from the history of computing, the generative "love-letters" that first appeared on the notice board of Manchester University's Computer Department in 1953 are similarly revealing. Predating the chatterbot *Eliza*, these computer-generated declarations were produced by a program written by the programmer Christopher Strachey, using the built-in random generator of the Manchester University Computer (the Ferranti Mark I), the earliest programmable computer (first functioning as a prototype in 1948). Artist David Link reconstructed a functional replica of the hardware and the original program, following meticulous research on the functional aspects but also speculating on why the programmer may have decided to generate love letters at all. The main program is relatively simple, using loops and a random variable to follow the sentence structure: "You are my — Adjective — Substantive," and "My — [Adjective] — Substantive — [Adverb] — Verb — Your — [Adjective] — Substantive."[38]

Some words are fixed and some optional, indicated by the square brackets; the program selects from the list of options—adjectives, adverbs, and verbs—and loops are configured to avoid repetition. The software could generate over 318 billion variations. In terms of effect, the dialogic structure is important too in setting up an exchange between "Me" (the program writer) and "You" (the human reader), such that you feel addressed directly—it *interpellates* you.

The resultant declarations suggest a surprising tenderness of expression that runs contrary to what we consider the standard functional outcomes of computational procedures (for commerce or war). Here is an example:

```
DEAR DARLING
    YOU ARE MY BEAUTIFUL RAPTURE. MY INFATUATION BEAUTIFULLY CLINGS TO
YOUR ADORABLE LUST. MY INFATUATION LUSTS FOR YOUR WISH. MY AMBITION
CURIOUSLY LIKES YOUR LOVE. YOU ARE MY DEAR EAGERNESS.
                                                  YOURS WISTFULLY
                                                   M. U. C.[39]
```

If computers could speak freely, is this what they would say? Is love reducible to a "recombinatory procedure"?[40] Surely not. On the one hand, as Link points out, it seems to portray a reductionist view of love, but on the other, love is also characterized by projection, and in this way fires the imagination. He explains this by quoting Goethe, who "once made the cynical suggestion that love-letters should be formulated in a completely cryptic way, so that the recipient could project whatever she liked into the text."[41] Moreover, cryptology aside, is the love letter reducible to the problem of memory like the Universal Machine, to be written, read, stored, and deleted like any other data? Once more, it is worth being reminded that people are not simply

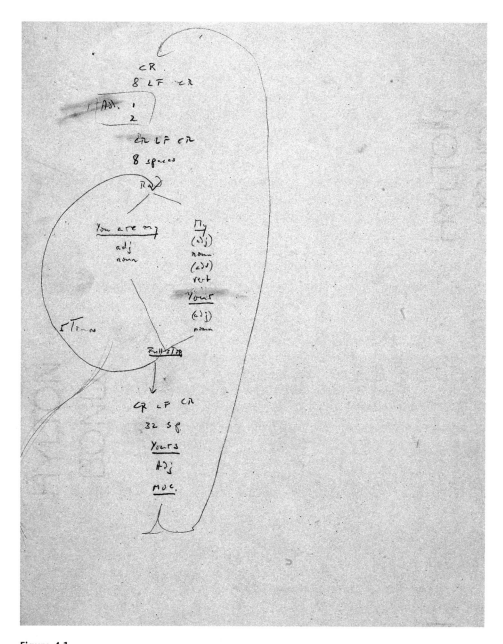

Figure 4.1
Schematic of Christopher Strachey's love letters program (1953). © The Bodleian Libraries, University of Oxford, CSAC 71.1.80/C.34.

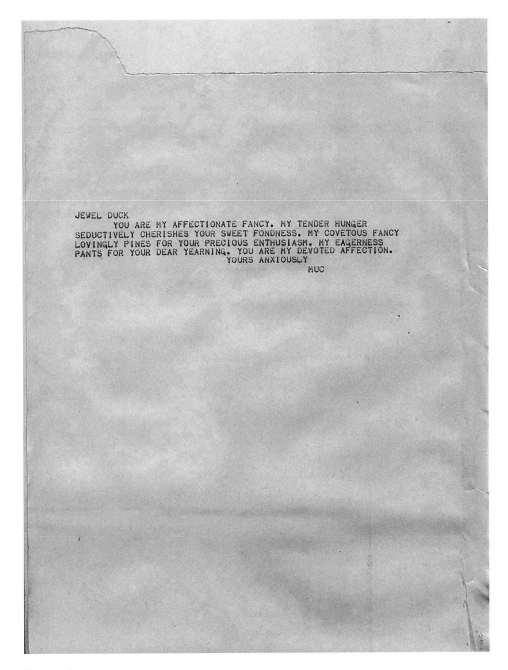

Figure 4.2
Image from David Link's *Loveletters_1.0* (2009). Image courtesy of David Link.

determined by such histories but are also involved in its very construction: both pro-grammed and able to program.

If love and tenderness are indeed neglected, as Berardi indicates, then we haven't recognized that love is preprogrammed, and that attempts to pervert this "truth" ultimately fail to interpellate. Indeed if running algorithms is a kind of "truth telling," as Link argues elsewhere,[42] then recognition holds a far more positive message than the hallucinations imposed by neoliberal markets, and the increased prominence of privatized technologies that deny access to source code. If human experience is ever more prescribed through scripts and programs like this, and which we have less and less access and attachment to, then the challenge for those making programs is to open up aesthetic and political possibilities of recombination and to liberate the imagination and desire from the market. Thankfully humans are not reducible to computational logic, but perhaps more importantly love was there all along, even with computer programs. But with little time for this realization, humans have become more and more distanced from the ability to communicate intimately with others.

Speech appears to have lost its power, along with the efficacy of human solidarity. The biopolitical dimension of this is key, as it addresses the ability of subjects to have a voice, one that connects to the expression of opinions in public and that is tied to subjective expression. Together these conditions operate as guiding concepts for con-temporary politics and for the ability to think and act in the world with any degree of thoughtfulness or effectiveness. Dolar explains how in Aristotle's *Politics*, the politi-cal is defined in terms of the distinction between mere voice (*phoné*) and speech (*logos*), the former common to all animals including the human animal, but the latter distin-guishing humans from other animals in their ability to articulate judgments in asso-ciation with others. This distinction (as Dolar further explains) is what Agamben is also referring to with his opposition between "bare life" (*zoe*), life in common with animals, and life in the community (*bios*), the commons and political life.[43] Each of these elements, however, is reciprocally embedded in the other and not simply exter-nal to it. Referring to Schmitt's view of sovereignty and the rule of exception, Agamben explains this as "the condition of being excluded through an exclusion, of being in relation to something from which one is excluded."[44]

For Dolar, this is an invitation to extend the analogy and think of the inclusion and exclusion of the voice in speech. Like bare life, the voice is both included and excluded in the political realm. This is a voice that is connected to politics and the essence of life itself, both within and beyond politics. It also connects usefully to the biopolitical dimension of technology in the development of speaking and thinking machines, or of telecommunications platforms where the voice is paradoxi-cally included and excluded at the same time. Dolar neatly takes this to represent the Hegelian move from "in-itself," in the case of the speaking machine, to "for-itself" in the thinking machine.[45] The voice stands as a figure for something that does not entirely compute and resists its capture, while retaining the possibility of free thinking.

What seem to be required are dynamic recombinations of speaking, thinking, and coding. To enable this, forms of totality have to be rejected, whether related to a view of the historical subject or to a view of program code that is deterministic or totalitarian, thus rupturing the relations between being programmed and programming. If the autonomy of intellectual labor from economic rule can alone save us from semiocapital, as Berardi states, then it needs recombining with the voice *and* code in recognition that both are always ready for action and at the same time ready to run out of control (like a live-coding performance). For it is this sense of incompleteness that drives transformational agency, and the ways in which human subjects retain the ability to modify their lived circumstances knowing their experiences to be incomplete. The recognition of the choice of action, already programmed but perhaps not knowingly so, confirms that both subjectivity and code recursively write their own instrumentation. Yet the subject is not simply preprogrammed like a machine but more like code in actively combining internal and external factors, standing between what is possible and what actually exists. Extending the move from in-itself to for-itself further, collective and networked intelligence open up the conditions of possibility for reinvention by embracing broader contingencies, to challenge overpowering forces that wish to close them down, encapsulate and subsume them.

If lived experience is ever more prescribed through scores, scripts, and programs, then the challenge for those making program scripts that underscore these procedures is to open up aesthetic and political possibilities of recombination and free the imagination to further use. Thus the performativity of code, in live coding or code acts, demonstrates the potential for collective intelligence and effective action. It proposes coding practices that have not only a body but also a body politic.

```python
#!/usr/bin/python

# (C) alex@slab.org
# Please edit and share.
# This program is free software: you can redistribute it and/or modify
# it under the terms of the GNU General Public License as published by
# the Free Software Foundation, either version 3 of the License, or
# (at your option) any later version.

import time, os, MultipartPostHandler, urllib2, cookielib
import libtorrent as lt

fs = lt.file_storage()
lt.add_files(fs, __file__)
t = lt.create_torrent(fs, 65536)
t.add_tracker("udp://tracker.openbittorrent.com:80", 0)
```

```
lt.set_piece_hashes(t, '.')
tf = lt.bencode(t.generate())

fh = open('me.torrent', 'wb')
fh.write(tf)
fh.close()

info = lt.torrent_info(lt.bdecode(lt.bencode(t.generate())))

opener = urllib2.build_opener(
    urllib2.HTTPCookieProcessor(cookielib.CookieJar()),
    MultipartPostHandler.MultipartPostHandler
    )

opener.open("http://runme.org/submit/",
        {'act': 'login',
         'email': 'torrentpy@mail.slab.org',
         'password': 'hjrvrs'
         }
        )

opener.open("http://runme.org/submit/",
        {'explicit_project_id': '974',
         'act': 'submit_software',
         'file_software': open('me.torrent')
         }
        )
ses = lt.session()
h = ses.add_torrent(info, "./")

state_str = ['queued', 'checking', 'downloading metadata',
             'downloading', 'finished', 'seeding', 'allocating']

while (1):
        s = h.status()
        print '%.2f%% complete (down: %.1f kb/s up: %.1f kB/s peers:
%d) %s' % (s.progress * 100, s.download_rate / 1000, s.upload_rate /
1000,
           s.num_peers, state_str[s.state])
       time.sleep(5)
```

Notes

0   Double Coding

1. For more on the Befunge programming language, see http://en.wikipedia.org/wiki/Befunge.

2. *The Hello World Collection*, compiled by Wolfram Roesler (with help from many people around the world), includes 421 "Hello world" programs in many more or less well-known programming languages, plus 63 human languages (available at http://roesler-ac.de/wolfram/hello.htm).

3. Referring to John 1:1: "In the beginning was the Word, and the Word was with God, and the Word was God."

4. Jonathan Rée, *I See a Voice: Language, Deafness and the Senses—A Philosophical History* (London: HarperCollins, 1999), 75–76. He is citing a passage from Genesis 11:1–9. Also of relevance here is the constructed language Volapük, created in 1879–1880 by Johann Martin Schleyer, who claimed that God had told him in a dream to create an international language. See Leo Findeisen, "Some Code to Die For: On the Birth of the Free Software Movement in 1887" (2003; available at http://www.monochrom.at/codetodiefor/).

5. Although the relationship between the study of machines and religious thinking is not the concern of this book, it is worth registering that Norbert Wiener identified commonalities in that machines must learn and reproduce in accordance with what he called the rules of the game, a game increasingly set by the dark forces of informational capitalism and the industrial-military complex. See Norbert Wiener, *God and Golem, Inc.* (Cambridge, MA: MIT Press, 1964).

6. "Twitspeak" is the vernacular form of language used with Twitter, such as the use of hashtags (see http://twitter.com/).

7. The Bodyfuck demo shows the physical exertion required to produce a short sequence of symbols (available at http://forum.openframeworks.cc/index.php?topic=2772.0).

8. Friedrich Kittler, "There Is No Software," in Timothy Druckrey, ed., *Electronic Culture* (New York: Aperture, 1996), 331–337 (available at http://www.ctheory.net/articles.aspx?id=74). Matthew Fuller's "It Looks Like You're Writing a Letter," in *Behind the Blip: Essays on the Culture of Software* (New York: Autonomedia, 2003), makes a similar reading through a close analysis of the word-processing software Microsoft Word, with a further link to the politics of work through the Office suite of programs.

9. Louis Althusser, "Ideology and Ideological State Apparatuses: Notes Toward an Investigation" (1969), in Slavoj Žižek, ed., *Mapping Ideology* (London: Verso, 1997), 131. To explain, "ideological

State apparatuses" include the family, schools, church, legal apparatus, political systems, trade unions, communications media, arts and culture, and so on, as distinct from the "repressive State apparatuses," the government, army, police, courts, prisons, and so on. Both function through repression and ideology, but the difference is that ideological State apparatuses, rather than acting predominantly by repression or violence, function through ideology and do so more covertly, such that people respond willingly.

10. Friedrich Kittler, "Code," in Matthew Fuller, ed., *Software Studies: A Lexicon* (Cambridge, MA: MIT Press, 2008).

11. Ibid., 41. More specifically, this is what Kittler refers to as the US Pentagon's imperial motto of C^4: namely, "command, control, communication, computers."

12. Moreover, the program both says something and does something at the same time and in the same place, and thus counters commonly held assumptions about language taking two main forms, in which speech privileges time over space and writing space over time.

13. Althusser, "Ideology and Ideological State Apparatuses."

14. Slavoj Žižek, *The Ticklish Subject: The Absent Centre of Political Ontology* (London: Verso, 1999), 60.

15. Judith Butler, *Excitable Speech: A Politics of the Performative* (London: Routledge, 1997).

16. Mladen Dolar, *A Voice and Nothing More* (Cambridge, MA: MIT Press, 2006), 3.

17. Butler, *Excitable Speech*, 15.

18. Althusser, "Ideology and Ideological State Apparatuses," 131. I have borrowed the idea of the allocation of an IP address from Brian Holmes's conference paper "Artistic Autonomy and the Communication Society," in *Diffusion: Collaborative Practice in Contemporary Art* (London: Tate Modern, 2003).

19. Butler, *Excitable Speech*, 26.

20. Brian Holmes, "Future Map: or, How the Cyborgs Learned to Stop Worrying and Love Surveillance," in *Continental Drift* (2007; available at http://brianholmes.wordpress.com/2007/09/09/future-map/).

21. Terry Winogrand and Fernando Flores, *Understanding Computers and Cognition: A New Foundation for Design* (Reading, MA: Addison-Wesley, 1987). Inke Arns also emphasized the analogy in "Read_Me, Run_Me, Execute_Me: Software and Its Discontents, or, It's the Performativity of Code, Stupid," in Olga Goriunova and Alexei Shulgin, eds., *Read_Me: Software Art and Cultures* (Aarhus: Digital Aesthetics Research Centre, University of Aarhus, 2004), 176–193.

22. The TopLap website, dedicated to live coding, also contains an evolving set of definitions and a draft manifesto (available at http://toplap.org/index.php?title=Main_Page).

23. For more on Rosetta Code, see http://rosettacode.org/wiki/Rosetta_Code.

24. For more on Instructionset, see http://instructionset.org/.

25. For instance, Mark Marino, in his article "Critical Code Studies" (2006), expresses "Hello world!" using Lisp and comments on its suitability as the language that was developed for artificial intelligence, thus encapsulating the imagined ability of machines to speak like humans. (Available at http://www.electronicbookreview.com/thread/electropoetics/codology?mode=print.)

26. Piet is an esoteric programming language written by David Morgan-Mar. His explanation of the Piet "Hello world!" program is available at http://www.retas.de/thomas/computer/programs/useless/piet/explain.html.

27. Kittler, "Code," 46.

28. Donald Knuth, *The Art of Computer Programming*, vol. 1, *Fundamental Algorithms* (Reading, MA: Addison-Wesley, 1981), v.

29. Ibid., xv–xvi.

30. N. Katherine Hayles, *Writing Machines* (Cambridge, MA: MIT Press, 2002), 25.

31. Roland Barthes, "The Death of the Author," in *Image, Music, Text* (London: Fontana, 1977), 142–148.

32. Heinz von Foerster, *Cybernetics of Cybernetics* (Urbana: University of Illinois, 1974).

33. Gregory Bateson, *Steps to an Ecology of Mind* (1971; Chicago: University of Chicago Press, 2000).

34. Gregory Bateson, *Mind and Nature: A Necessary Unity* (Cresskill, NJ: Hampton Press, 1979). Thanks to David Dunn for this reference.

35. Available at http://beehive.temporalimage.com/content_apps34/mez/0.html.

36. For a good example of an entry in the International Obfuscated C Code Contest, see an uncompiled C program that is self-referential, reproducing the logic of code as a portrait (available at http://www.Ioccc.org/2000/dhyang.c).

37. Amy Alexander, deprogramming.us (available at http://deprogramming.us/prozac.html).

38. Alan Kay and Adele Goldberg, "Personal Dynamic Media," in Noah Wardrip-Fruin and Nick Montfort, eds., *The New Media Reader* (Cambridge, MA: MIT Press, 2003), 393–404.

39. Here I am paraphrasing Henry Giroux's much-used questions: "Who speaks, under what conditions, on behalf of whom?," in *Living Dangerously: Multiculturalism and the Politics of Difference* (New York: Peter Lang, 1993).

40. Dolar, *A Voice and Nothing More*, 84.

41. Walter J. Ong, *Orality and Literacy: The Technologizing of the Word* (1982; London: Routledge, 2002), 8.

42. bell hooks, "Talking Back," in Russell Ferguson, Martha Gever, et al., eds., *Out There: Marginalization and Contemporary Cultures* (Cambridge, MA: MIT Press, 1989).

43. Georges Bataille, *The Accursed Share*, vol. 1, trans. Robert Hurley (New York: Zone Books, 1991). Excess is elementary to Bataille's notion of "general economy" where expenditure (waste, sacrifice, or destruction) is considered more fundamental than the economies of production and utilities.

44. Ian Bogost, *Unit Operations: An Approach to Videogame Criticism* (Cambridge, MA: MIT Press, 2004), making reference to the work of Graham Harman in particular and what has become known as "speculative realism," also associated with Ray Brassier, Iain Hamilton Grant, and Quentin Meillassoux.

45. Alain Badiou, *Number and Numbers* (Cambridge: Polity Press, 2008), 1. Numbers may have been somewhat repressed in Continental philosophy at the time of Badiou's writing (in French, 1990), but the same cannot be said now. The present financial crisis can perhaps be read as the return of the repressed.

46. Ong, *Orality and Literacy*.

47. Boris Groys, *The Communist Postscript* (London: Verso, 2009), xvi.

48. For instance, Norie Neumark, Ross Gibson, and Theo van Leeuwen, eds., *Voice: Vocal Aesthetics in Digital Arts and Media* (Cambridge, MA: MIT Press, 2010); and even the film *Speaking in Code* by Amy Grill (2009), although this is about getting lost in techno music.

49. Hannah Arendt, *The Human Condition* (1958; Chicago: University of Chicago Press, 1998).

50. Paolo Virno, *A Grammar of the Multitude: For an Analysis of Contemporary Forms of Life*, trans. Isabella Bertoletti, James Cascaito, and Andrea Casson (New York: Semiotext(e), 2004).

51. Christopher M. Kelty, *Two Bits: The Cultural Significance of Free Software* (Durham: Duke University Press, 2008).

52. Franco "Bifo" Berardi, *The Soul at Work: From Alienation to Autonomy* (Los Angeles: Semiotext(e), 2009). Berardi invokes the soul to examine contemporary productive forms that put the soul to work (in a materialist sense).

53. The "grain of the voice" is what Barthes calls the individual "voice-magic," imparted by the "very precise space of the encounter between a language and a voice." Roland Barthes, "The Grain of the Voice," in *Image, Music, Text*, 181. The music industry tries to commodify this "grain."

54. It is interesting to note that a function to calculate pi can be written; the issue is that it would never return the value. If running indefinitely, a Turing machine would be able to output it all, as it has infinite memory.

55. Groys, *The Communist Postscript*, xvii.

56. Nick Couldry, *Why Voice Matters: Culture and Politics after Neoliberalism* (London: Sage, 2010), 3.

57. Echoed in the phrase "words made flesh," the title of Florian Cramer's *Words Made Flesh: Code, Culture, Imagination* (Rotterdam: Piet Zwart Institute, 2005), 125 (available at http://pzwart.wdka.hro.nl/mdr/research/fcramer/wordsmadeflesh/).

58. "His Master's Voice" is the famous gramophone trademark, based on an 1899 painting by Francis Barraud, showing the dog Nipper listening obediently to his owner's phonograph (circa 1930).

1   Vocable Code

1. Drawing upon Jonathan Rée's *I See a Voice: Language, Deafness and the Senses—A Philosophical History* (London: HarperCollins, 1999), we previously speculated whether code could be seen to work in a similar way to poetry by acknowledging the conditions of its own making—its *poiesis*. Geoff Cox, Alex McLean, and Adrian Ward, "The Aesthetics of Generative Code," paper delivered at Generative Art 00, international conference, Politecnico di Milano (2000; available at http://www.generative.net/papers/aesthetics/index.html).

2. Geoff Cox, Alex McLean, and Adrian Ward, "Coding Praxis: Reconsidering the Aesthetics of Code," in Olga Goriunova and Alexei Shulgin, eds., *Read_Me: Software Art and Cultures* (Aarhus: Digital Aesthetics Research Centre, University of Aarhus, 2004), 161–174.

3. Franco Berardi read the source code of the virus at the D-I-N-A (Digital Is Not Analog) digital art festival in 2001 (available at http://www.digitalcraft.org/iloveyou/loveletter_reading.htm). Another example that will be mentioned in chapter 2 is radioqualia's *Free Radio Linux* (2001), in which the source code of the Linux kernel was webcast over the Internet using a speech synthesizer. (See http://www.radioqualia.net/documentation/frl/index.html.)

4. Kurt Schwitters, *Poems, Performance Pieces, Proses, Plays, Poetics*, ed. and trans. Jerome Rothenberg and Pierre Joris (Cambridge, MA: Exact Change, 2002), xvii.

5. Excerpt from the introduction to the *Ursonate* by Kurt Schwitters (1932), *Merz*, 24 (available at http://www.ubu.com/historical/schwitters/ursonate.html).
6. We know this from Ferdinand de Saussure's lectures, later published as *Course in General Linguistics* (1916; available at http://www.marxists.org/reference/subject/philosophy/works/fr/saussure.htm).
7. Ibid.
8. This line of thinking is exemplified by Fredric Jameson in *The Prison-House of Language: A Critical Account of Structuralism and Russian Formalism* (Princeton: Princeton University Press, 1972), where he looks for the structures of consciousness itself.
9. This is something that Tzvetan Todorov explained in *Grammaire du Décaméron*: "Every work, every novel, tells through its fabric of events the story of its own creation, its own history . . . the meaning of a work lies in its telling itself, its speaking of its own existence." Quoted in Terence Hawkes, *Structuralism and Semiotics* (1977; London: Methuen, 1986), 100.
10. Noam Chomsky, *Syntactic Structures* (1957; The Hague: Mouton, 1972), 106.
11. Douglas R. Hofstadter, *Gödel, Escher, Bach: An Eternal Golden Braid* (1979; London: Penguin, 2000), 495. He also uses the example of Escher's hands drawing hands already mentioned in the introduction. A further example is *prozac.pl*, also cited in the introduction.
12. In the older tradition of computer art or generative art from the 1960s and 1970s (as distinguished from a more contemporary understanding of software art), Max Bense's theory of "generative aesthetics" was influenced by Chomsky's work on generative grammar. Max Bense, "The Projects of Generative Aesthetics," in Jasia Reichardt, ed., *Cybernetics, Art, and Ideas* (London: Studio Vista, 1971); available at http://www.computerkunst.org/Bense_Manifest.pdf.
13. N. Katherine Hayles, *Writing Machines* (Cambridge, MA: MIT Press, 2002), 6.
14. Friedrich Kittler's observation is much quoted: that to understand today's culture requires knowledge of a natural language and an artificial language. In a similar vein, Douglas Rushkoff, in *Program or Be Programmed: Ten Commands for a Digital Age* (Berkeley, CA: Soft Skull Press, 2011), argues that in order to participate fully in contemporary democracy we all now need to learn to program, to avoid being programmed.
15. Friedrich Kittler, "There Is No Software," in Timothy Druckrey, ed., *Electronic Culture* (New York: Aperture, 1996), 332.
16. Ibid. Kittler is referring to his own previous work, "Protected Mode," in Ute Bernhardt and Ingo Ruhmann, eds., *Computer, Macht und Gegenwehr. InformatikerInnen für eine andere Informatik* (Bonn: FIfF, 1991), 34–44.
17. This ideological distinction will be returned to in chapter 3, which further explores the paradoxes around technology's social potential.
18. Eric S. Raymond, *The Art of UNIX Programming* (Boston: Addison-Wesley, 2004), 8. It should be noted, however, that Raymond's idea of openness does not stretch beyond UNIX as he has made himself gatekeeper of *The Hacker's Dictionary*, changing the very definition of programmer culture to reflect his own free-market ideology. (Available at http://www.ntk.net/2003/06/06/.)
19. Raymond, *The Art of UNIX Programming*, 25. The phrase alludes to Einstein's soundbite, "Everything should be made as simple as possible, but no simpler."
20. Florian Cramer, "Exe.cut[up]able statements: The Insistence of Code," in Gerfried Stocker and Christine Schöpf, eds., *Code: The Language of Our Time* (Linz: Ars Electronica; Ostfildern-Ruit:

Hatje Cantz, 2003). He is referring to Barthes's *S/Z: An Essay*. In Cramer's view the lasting importance of Kittler lies in his stress on technomaterialism.

21. Ibid., 102.

22. Florian Cramer, "Concepts, Notations, Software Art," in Olga Goriunova and Alexei Shulgin, eds., *Software Art: Thoughts*, catalog of the Read_me Festival 1.2 (Moscow: Rosizo, State Centre for Museums and Exhibitions, 2002), 18–24.

23. The original score, Alvin Lucier's *I am sitting in a room (for voice on tape)* (1969), is available at http://ubu.artmob.ca/sound/source/Lucier-Alvin_Sitting.mp3.

24. For instance, Mikhail Bahktin's concept of "heteroglossia" (literally "different speech-ness") describes the conflict between different types of speech, such as those emanating from author, characters, narrator, etc. See Mikhail Bakhtin, "Discourse in the Novel," in Bakhtin, *The Dialogic Imagination: Four Essays*, ed. Michael Holquist (Austin: University of Texas Press, 1981), 259–422.

25. See Steven Feuerstein, *Oracle PL/SQL Programming* (Cambridge, MA: O'Reilly, 1997).

26. On his website Feuerstein explains: "I decided to use non-traditional examples. Instead of HR and order entry, I talked about excessive CEO compensation, union busting, war crimes—all sorts of truly inspiring examples. Hmmm. Anyway, lots of people liked it, lots of people hated." (Available at http://www.stevenfeuerstein.com/books/content/merging-technology-and-politics.)

27. Harwood, in *XXXXX* (Berlin and London: Openmute Press, 2006), 120–127. Note that Harwood is the preferred name of the artist Graham Harwood.

28. Larry Wall, "Perl Culture," in *Programming Perl* (Sebastopol, CA: O'Reilly, 2001); available at http://docstore.mik.ua/orelly/perl/prog3/ch27_02.htm. Also see Geoff Cox and Adrian Ward, "Perl," in Matthew Fuller, ed., *Software Studies: A Lexicon* (Cambridge, MA: MIT Press, 2008).

29. Hayles, *Writing Machines*, 107.

30. N. Katherine Hayles, *My Mother Was a Computer* (Chicago: University of Chicago Press, 2005), 56.

31. Ibid., 58.

32. Walter J. Ong, *Orality and Literacy: The Technologizing of the Word* (1982; London: Routledge, 2002), 7.

33. George Lakoff and Mark Johnson, *Philosophy in the Flesh: The Embodied Mind and Its Challenge to Western Thought* (New York: HarperCollins, 1999).

34. The work of Paul Dourish is one obvious example, for instance his *Where the Action Is: The Foundations of Embodied Interaction* (Cambridge, MA: MIT Press, 2001).

35. For instance, Owen Holland takes an embodied approach to representation in software using robotics, making the case that consciousness itself is an agent's simulation of itself interacting with a simulation of its environment, in Owen Holland, ed., *Machine Consciousness* (Exeter: Imprint Academic, 2003).

36. Edsger W. Dijkstra, "A Review of the 1977 Turing Award Lecture by John Backus" (1977; available at http://www.cs.utexas.edu/users/EWD/transcriptions/EWD06xx/EWD692.html).

37. Edward A. Lee, "Computing Needs Time," *Communications of the ACM* 52 (5): 70–79 (2009; available at http://cacm.acm.org/magazines/2009/5/24649-computing-needs-time/fulltext).

38. Rée, *I See a Voice*. His concern is to highlight that the logic of this informs the historical maltreatment of those that cannot speak, as animals outside the human world of normal language (the so-called "deaf and dumb").

39. Ibid., 67.

40. For instance, taking up the challenge in 2001–2002 and following Kempelen's instructions closely, Jakob Scheid translated the use of traditional materials to digital computer methods (see http://klangmaschinen.ima.or.at/db/pv.php?table=Object&id=2011&lang=).

41. Brigitte Felderer, "Orality," in *Zauberhafte Klangmaschinen: Von der Sprechmaschine bis zur Soundkarte* (Hainburg: IMA Institut für Medienarchäologie, Schott Music, 2008), 92. The speaking machine can still be seen in the Deutsches Museum, Munich.

42. See Wikipedia entry, available at http://en.wikipedia.org/wiki/Wolfgang_von_Kempelen%27s_Speaking_Machine.

43. Rée, *I See a Voice*, 258.

44. Ong, *Orality and Literacy*, 86.

45. See http://www.omniglot.com/writing/korean.htm.

46. Rée, *I See a Voice*, 262.

47. George Bernard Shaw, *Pygmalion* (1916). Also see Ovid's *Metamorphoses*, book X.

48. Alan Turing, "Computing Machinery and Intelligence" (1950), in Noah Wardrip-Fruin and Nick Montfort, eds., *The New Media Reader* (Cambridge, MA: MIT Press, 2003), 49–64.

49. See http://www.captcha.net/.

50. John R. Searle, "Minds, Brains, and Programs," *Behavioral and Brain Sciences* 3 (1980): 417.

51. Ibid., 418.

52. Diane Proudfoot, "Wittgenstein's Anticipation of the Chinese Room," in John Preston and Mark Bishop, eds., *Views into the Chinese Room: New Essays on Searle and Artificial Intelligence* (Oxford: Clarendon Press, 2002), 168.

53. Ibid., 168–169, citing Wittgenstein's *Philosophical Investigations* (1953).

54. Proudfoot, "Wittgenstein's Anticipation of the Chinese Room," 177–178.

55. John R. Searle, "Twenty-One Years in the Chinese Room," in Preston and Bishop, *Views into the Chinese Room*, 56.

56. Ibid. With this statement, Searle is arguing that Turing machines rely on abstract mathematical processes but not on energy transfer like some other machines; and one might extrapolate that the discourse around artificial life reinvigorates the fantasies of artificial intelligence in this way. Merely increasing computer capacity does not mean machine consciousness is any closer but perhaps only that the fantasies become stronger, as artificial intelligence morphs into the discourse around artificial life and the messier biocomputational "wet" realm of living cells.

57. Description of the articulatory synthesis package in Praat. See http://www.fon.hum.uva.nl/praat/manual/Articulatory_synthesis.html.

58. Such as Apple Computer's MacInTalk released in 1984, later combined with a range of sample voices, which by 2010 include those for Mac OS X 10.5 (Leopard) with realistic-sounding breaths between sentences.

59. Hayles, *My Mother Was a Computer*, 39. See also Jay Bolter and Richard Grusin, *Remediation: Understanding New Media* (Cambridge, MA: MIT Press, 1999).

60. Hayles, *My Mother Was a Computer*, 45.

61. Ibid., 49.

62. J. L. Austin, *How to Do Things with Words* (Cambridge, MA: Harvard University Press, 1975). The William James Lectures (of 1955) were based on earlier lectures at Oxford, "Words and Deeds" (1952–1954), and prefigured the BBC lecture "Performative Utterances" (1959).

63. Ibid., 6.

64. Ibid., 109.

65. Alan Cienki, "Why Study Metaphor and Gesture?," in Alan Cienki and Cornelia Müller, eds., *Metaphor and Gesture* (Amsterdam: John Benjamins, 2008), 5–25 (available at http://benjamins.com/cgi-bin/t_bookview.cgi?bookid=GS%203).

66. See Alex McLean's notes on *Vocable Synthesis* (2008) and video demonstrations (available at http://yaxu.org/category/vocable/).

67. Available at http://www.virtual-circuit.org/audio/sound/ethno/Salute.html.

68. Alex McLean and Geraint Wiggins, "Words, Movement and Timbre," conference paper, NIME09, Pittsburgh (3–6 June 2009); available at http://doc.gold.ac.uk/~ma503am/writing/nime09.pdf.

69. See Alex McLean's *Babble*, an online version commissioned by Arnolfini (2008; available at http://project.arnolfini.org.uk/babble/).

70. Alex McLean's notes (2009; available at http://yaxu.org/metaphors-of-javadoc/).

71. Austin, *How to Do Things with Words*, 10.

72. Judith Butler explains excess as more like a loss of context than like context, in her book *Excitable Speech: A Politics of the Performative* (London: Routledge, 1997), 4. For her purpose, this is where violent speech acts reside.

73. The chapter has tried to signal this in its attention to oral and written forms. Ong says something similar in refering to a "text-act" (a term he takes from Winifred B. Horner), in *Orality and Literacy*, 167.

74. See Georges Bataille, *The Accursed Share*, trans. Robert Hurley (New York: Zone Books, 1988–1991).

2   Code Working

1. Maurizio Lazzarato, "Immaterial Labor," in Paolo Virno and Michael Hardt, eds., *Radical Thought in Italy: A Potential Politics* (Minneapolis: University of Minnesota Press, 1996), 132–146.

2. Alan Sondheim, "Introduction to Codework," *American Book Review* 22 (6) (2001): 1–2; available at http://www.litline.org/ABR/issues/Volume22/Issue6/sondheim.pdf.

3. Félix Guattari, *Chaosophy*, ed. Sylvère Lotringer (New York: Semiotext(e), 1995).

4. Graham Harwood, "Class Library," in Matthew Fuller, ed., *Software Studies: A Lexicon* (Cambridge, MA: MIT Press, 2008), 37–39.

5. The concept of "general intellect," drawn from Marx's early writing, is a key one for autonomist Marxism, and in particular for the work of Paolo Virno which will be referred to later in the book. See Karl Marx, "Fragment on Machines," in *Grundrisse: Foundations of the Critique of Political Economy (Rough Draft)* (Harmondsworth: Penguin, 1981), 705–706.

6. Hannah Arendt, "Labor, Work, Action" (1964), in *The Portable Hannah Arendt* (New York: Penguin 2000), 167–181.

7. Ian Bogost, "Procedural Rhetoric," in *Persuasive Games: The Expressive Power of Videogames* (Cambridge, MA: MIT Press, 2007), 5. Bogost develops the idea of "unit operations" from this to describe an object-oriented approach (object-oriented ontology, in terms of both programming and philosophy), but the main issue here is to stress that computational representation and other cultural processes are bound together.

8. This is an idea I have previously explored through the phrase "software has no history," in a paper with that title delivered at re:place, Second International Conference on the Histories of Media, Art, Science and Technology, Haus der Kulturen der Welt, Berlin (2007; available at http://www.mediaarthistory.org/?page_id=25). The ironic phrase is borrowed from John Roberts, ed., *Art Has No History! The Making and Unmaking of Modern Art* (London: Verso, 1994). In turn, he borrows it from Louis Althusser's "Ideology Has No History" (of 1969); Althusser was referring to Marx and Engels's *The German Ideology* (of 1845–1846). When Althusser claimed that "ideology has no history," he was expressing what he perceived to be its unchanging structure, to indicate that ideology is pure illusion produced by those in power; but he also meant that its sense of history is a mere reflection of real history—in that it has "no history of its own." See Louis Althusser, "Ideology and Ideological State Apparatuses: Notes Toward an Investigation," in Slavoj Žižek, ed., *Mapping Ideology* (London: Verso, 1997), 122.

9. Pall Thayer, *Repeating History* (2009; available at http://pallit.lhi.is/microcodes/contr.php?code_id=28). One of a series of his "microcodes," this is inspired by *The Wheel of the Devil* (MTAA and Ed Halter) and *historic_loop* (James Morris).

10. Karl Marx, "The Eighteenth Brumaire of Louis Bonaparte" (1852; available at http://www.marxists.org/archive/marx/works/1852/18th-brumaire/ch01.htm).

11. Roy Bhaskar, Andrew Collier, and Alan Norrie, "Dialectic and Dialectical Critical Realism," in Margaret Archer, Roy Bhaskar, Andrew Collier, Tony Lawson, and Alan Norrie, eds., *Critical Realism: Essential Readings* (London: Routledge, 1998).

12. Georg W. F. Hegel, *The Phenomenology of Mind* (1807; New York: Harper and Row, 1967). For a fuller discussion of Marx's adaptation, see Georg Lukács, *History and Class Consciousness: Studies in Marxism* (1922; Cambridge, MA: MIT Press, 1976).

13. It should be said that this is also the project of "media archaeology": to present an account of nonlinear historical and technological development that is rather different from narrativized versions (see Wolfgang Ernst and Friedrich Kittler). Instead of linear history, something far more recursive is presented.

14. Slavoj Žižek, "Hegel's 'Logic of Essence' as a Theory of Ideology," in *The Žižek Reader*, ed. Elizabeth Wright and Edmond Wright (Oxford: Blackwell, 1999), 225–250.

15. Heinz von Foerster, *Cybernetics of Cybernetics* (Urbana: University of Illinois, 1974). Associated with von Foerster among others, second-order cybernetics investigates cybernetics with awareness that the investigators are part of the system, and of the importance of self-referentiality, and self-organization.

16. Žižek, "Hegel's 'Logic of Essence' as a Theory of Ideology."

17. Bhaskar, Collier, and Norrie, "Dialectic and Dialectical Critical Realism," xiv.

18. It is interesting to note that Kittler also refers to the principle of "recursive history," in John Armitage, "From Discourse Networks to Cultural Mathematics: An Interview with Friedrich A. Kittler," *Theory, Culture and Society* 23 (17) (2006): 33; available at http://tcs.sagepub.com/content/23/7-8/17.

19. See also Geoff Cox, *Antithesis: The Dialectics of Software Art* (Aarhus: Digital Aesthetic Research Centre, Aarhus University, 2010; first written in 2006 as a University of Plymouth doctoral thesis).

20. Bhaskar, Collier, and Norrie, "Dialectic and Dialectical Critical Realism," 600.

21. Douglas R. Hofstadter, *Gödel, Escher, Bach: An Eternal Golden Braid* (1979; London: Penguin, 2000), 689. Hofstadter also refers to M. C. Escher's lithograph *Drawing Hands* (1948), where "that which draws, and that which is drawn—turn back on each other."

22. Hofstadter coins the term "quine" in honor of Willard Van Orman Quine, an influential mathematician and philosopher. Extensive notes by David Madore on quines are available at http://www.madore.org/~david/computers/quine.html.

23. Alex McLean's *forkbomb.pl* (2002; available at http://runme.org/project/+forkbomb/).

24. deprogramming.us, *forkwar.pl* (2003; available at http://deprogramming.us/forkwar.html).

25. Wendy Hui Kyong Chun identifies some of the reductive understandings of the permanence of memory that storage encourages in "The Enduring Ephemeral, or the Future Is a Memory," paper delivered at re:place, Second International Conference on the Histories of Media, Art, Science and Technology, Haus der Kulturen der Welt, Berlin (2007; available at http://www.mediaarthistory.org/?page_id=25). Also see Chun, *Programmed Visions: Software and Memory* (Cambridge, MA: MIT Press, 2011).

26. This view of inscription to account for the different ways that data is processed historically is what Kittler refers to as "discourse networks." See Friedrich Kittler, *Discourse Networks 1800/1900*, trans. M. Metteer and C. Cullens (Stanford: Stanford University Press, 1990). (The German title of his book, *Aufschreibesysteme* [inscription systems], was first used by Daniel Paul Schreber in his *Memoirs of My Nervous Illness* [1903] to designate how strange heavenly powers were tracking and recording his every move.)

27. Norbert Wiener commented that the accomplishments of artificial intelligence were as "fraudulent" as the chess-playing machine; see his *Cybernetics: or, Control and Communication in the Animal and the Machine* (1948; Cambridge, MA: MIT Press, 1965), 165.

28. Walter Benjamin, "On the Concept of History," in Benjamin, *Selected Writings*, vol. 4, *1938–1940*, ed. Howard Eiland and Michael W. Jennings (Cambridge, MA: Belknap Press, 2003). First written in French and often translated as "Theses on the Philosophy of History," the essay is well known for its reference to the allegorical figure of the angel of history, imagined from the painting *Angelus Novus* by Paul Klee, that wants to gather up the wreckage of history but cannot do this because of the ideological forces at work. Esther Leslie cites a statement by Adorno (in a 1962 radio lecture) who insists that Benjamin's angel is not only the angel of history but the angel of the machine. Her translation of Benjamin's opening passage follows:

The story is told of an automaton constructed in such a way that it could respond to each move in a game of chess with a countermove that ensured him victory. A puppet in Turkish attire, and with a hookah in his mouth, sat in front of a chessboard placed on a large table. A system of mirrors created the illusion of a table transparent from all sides. Actually a hunchback dwarf, who was an expert chess player, sat inside and guided the puppet's hand by means of strings. One can imagine a philosophical counterpart to this device. The puppet known as 'historical materialism' is always supposed to win. It can easily be a match for anyone if it ropes in the services of theology, which today, as the story goes, is small and ugly and must, as it is, keep out of sight.

Esther Leslie, *Walter Benjamin: Overpowering Conformism* (London: Pluto, 2000), 172.

29. The "automaton stripped naked" is the description by Karl Gottlieb von Windisch. That someone was hidden was first suggested by Henri Decremps and embellished by Joseph Friedrich Freiherr zu Racknitz, in a pamphlet of 1789. Both are cited in Gaby Wood's "An Unreasonable Game," in *Living Dolls* (London: Faber and Faber, 2002), 90.

30. Ibid., 72. Poe is writing for the *Southern Literary Messenger*; see also his essay "Maelzel's Chess Player," in *The Complete Tales and Poems of Edgar Allan Poe* (New York: Vintage, 1975).

31. Mladen Dolar, *A Voice and Nothing More* (Cambridge, MA: MIT Press, 2006).

32. Jonathan Rée, *I See a Voice: Language, Deafness and the Senses—A Philosophical History* (London: HarperCollins, 1999), 253–254.

33. Dolar, *A Voice and Nothing More*, 9.

34. Ibid., 11.

35. "Social factory" is another term developed within the *operaismo* and autonomist traditions, and implies that the power relations deployed in the factory also impact life outside the factory, and vice versa.

36. Marx, *Grundrisse: Foundations of the Critique of Political Economy (Rough Draft)*.

37. Amazon.com, Mechanical Turk (available at http://www.mturk.com/).

38. Trebor Scholz, "On MTurk, Some Examples of Exploitation" (2009; available at http://www.collectivate.net/journalisms/).

39. Aaron Koblin, *The Sheep Market* (2006; available at http://www.aaronkoblin.com/work/thesheepmarket/). It cannot go unnoticed that Koblin is both an artist known for his innovative uses of crowdsourcing and also currently Creative Director of the Data Arts Team at Google Creative Lab. His biography is available at http://www.aaronkoblin.com/info.html.

40. Antonio Negri, *Marx beyond Marx: Lessons on the Grundrisse*, ed. Jim Fleming, trans. Harry Cleaver, Michael Ryan, and Maurizio Viano (New York: Autonomedia/Pluto, 1991), 77.

41. Lazzarato, "Immaterial Labor," 132–146.

42. Franco "Bifo" Berardi, *The Soul at Work: From Alienation to Autonomy*, trans. Francesca Cadel and Giuseppina Mecchia (Los Angeles: Semiotext(e), 2009).

43. Ibid., 22–23.

44. By workerism (*operaismo* in Italian), I am referring to the 1960s Italian political movement that later developed into autonomism or autonomist Marxism. See "Autonomia: Post-political Politics," *Semiotext(e)* 3 (3) (1980).

45. Mario Tronti, "The Strategy of Refusal" (1965), in "Autonomia: Post-political Politics," 29.

46. The reference is to Aristotle's *On the Soul*; see *On the Soul and On Memory and Recollection*, trans. Joe Sachs (Santa Fe: Green Lion Press, 2001).

47. Marx, *Grundrisse: Foundations of the Critique of Political Economy (Rough Draft)*, 705–706.

48. Tiziana Terranova, "Free Labor: Producing Culture for the Digital Economy," *Social Text* 18 (2) (2000): 33–58.

49. See Marcel Mauss, *The Gift: Forms and Functions of Exchange in Archaic Societies*, trans. Ian Cunnison (London: Cohen and West, 1970).

50. Terranova, "Free Labor," 38.

51. Maurizio Lazzarato, "Forms of Production and Circulation of Knowledge," in Josephine Bosma et al., eds., *Readme! Filtered by Nettime: ASCII Culture and the Revenge of Knowledge* (New York: Autonomedia, 1999), 162. Tarde also suggests that the value of goods will become increasingly dependent on public perceptions or what he calls "inter-subjective communion," which reflects the concept of networked intelligence. Cited in Adam Avidsson and Elanor Colleoni, "Value in Informational Capitalism and on the Internet: A Reply to Christian Fuchs," *Social Science Research Network* (February 28, 2011); available at http://papers.ssrn.com/sol3/papers.cfm?abstract_id=1772975.

52. Robert Luxembourg, *The Conceptual Crisis of Private Property as a Crisis in Practice* (2003; available at http://rolux.net/crisis/index.php?crisis=documentation). Robert Luxembourg is a pseudonym for the artist Sebastian Lütgert.

53. *The Matrix*, film directed by Larry and Andy Wachowski (1999).

54. Michael Hardt and Antonio Negri, *Empire* (Cambridge, MA: Harvard University Press, 2000).

55. The gesture follows the logic of earlier works by Project Gnutenberg and the production of free software to allow for the covert distribution of copyrighted materials. Project Gnutenberg (combining Gutenberg and GNU, and a parody of Project Gutenberg) is unsurprisingly no longer online.

56. Richard Stallman, "Why Software Should Not Have Owners" (1994; available at http://www.gnu.org/philosophy/why-free.html).

57. Creative Commons, available at http://www.creativecommons.org/.

58. The counterargument is that it is necessary to use legal instruments and language as all human activity is affected by law, and that only in this way can rights and freedoms be protected. But this still seems based on the central paradox that the law is required to undo damage that it is complicit in creating in the first place.

59. Available at http://creativecommons.org/publicdomain/zero/1.0/.

60. Cited in Dmytri Kleiner, *The Telekommunist Manifesto*, Network Notebooks 03 (Amsterdam: Institute of Network Cultures, 2010), 43; available at http://www.telekommunisten.net/the-telekommunist-manifesto.

61. Rasmus Fleischer, "Kopimi," in Stian Rødven Eide, ed., *Free Beer 1.0* (Göteborg: FSCONS, 2009), 90. Piratbyrån interestingly describe their project as an ongoing conversation.

62. Kleiner, *The Telekommunist Manifesto*, 28.

63. Negation of negation is explained by Žižek as the separation of the "negated system's 'real' death from its 'symbolic' death . . . the system has to die twice." See Slavoj Žižek, *The Ticklish Subject: The Absent Centre of Political Ontology* (London: Verso, 1999), 72. Or to put it in straightforward Marxist terms: producers take over the means of production, but at this first stage it remains within the confines of private ownership; this first stage has to be further negated to abolish the whole principle of private ownership of the means of production.

64. Kleiner, *The Telekommunist Manifesto*, 10–12.

65. Referring to David Ricardo's *On the Principles of Political Economy and Taxation* of 1817.

66. Paolo Virno, *Multitude: Between Innovation and Negation*, trans. Isabella Bertoletti, James Cascaito, and Andrea Casson (New York: Semiotext(e), 2008), 50.

67. Kleiner, *The Telekommunist Manifesto*, 15.

68. Available at http://www.thimbl.net/.

69. The concept and source code are explained in more detail on the website (http://www.thimbl.net/), and further background is provided in Dmytri Kleiner's blog entry, "#Thimbl, Social Media Week, @dsearls and Economic Fiction as a Performative Artwork" (4 October 2011; available at http://www.dmytri.info/thimbl-social-media-week-dsearls-and-economic-fiction-as-a-performative-artwork/). Also see https://github.com/telekommunisten.

70. Kleiner, *The Telekommunist Manifesto*, 19. The point was first made in collaboration with Brian Wyrick in "Info-Enclosure 2.0," *Web 2.0: Man's Best Friendster?*, *Mute* 2 (4) (January 2007); available at http://www.metamute.org/Web-2.0-Mans-bestfriendster/.

71. Kleiner, "#Thimbl, Social Media Week, @dsearls and Economic Fiction as a Performative Artwork."

72. Ibid.

73. See Telekommunisten's website (http://www.telekommunisten.net/) for details of other projects in this series, such as *deadSwap* and *R15N*.

74. Guattari, *Chaosophy*.

75. Karl Marx, *Capital*, vol. 1, trans. Ben Fowkes (1867; Harmondsworth: Penguin, 1990), 492.

76. Ibid., 503.

77. The term "robot" was allegedly first used by Karel Čapek in his play *Rossum's Universal Robots* (Prague, 1921), drawing upon the Czech term *robota* which literally means "forced work or labor." In the play's scenario, a factory that builds artificial agents is eventually taken over by them and the whole of humanity destroyed.

78. Guattari, *Chaosophy*, 142.

79. Ibid., 19.

80. Arendt, "Labor, Work, Action."

81. Hannah Arendt, *The Human Condition* (1958; Chicago: University of Chicago Press, 1998), 225.

82. Ibid., 229.

83. Arendt, "Labor, Work, Action," 136. Arendt points out that most European languages make similar distinctions: *arbeiten* and *werken* in German; *laborare* and *fabricari* in Latin; *ponein* and *ergazesthai* in Greek.

84. Arendt, *The Human Condition*, 229–230.

85. Ibid., 167.

86. Ibid., 169.

87. Ibid., 170.

88. Arendt, "Labor, Work, Action," 175.

89. Paolo Virno, *A Grammar of the Multitude: For an Analysis of Contemporary Forms of Life*, trans. Isabella Bertoletti, James Cascaito, and Andrea Casson (New York: Semiotext(e), 2004), 50–51.

90. Ibid., 51.

91. Ibid., 52. Aristotle, *Nicomachean Ethics* (325 BC), in John Cottingham, ed. and trans., *Western Philosophy: An Anthology* (Oxford: Blackwell, 1996).

92. Giorgio Agamben, *Means without Ends: Notes on Politics*, trans. Vincenzo Binetti and Cesare Casarino (Minneapolis: University of Minnesota Press, 2000), 57.

93. Ibid., 117.

94. Aristotle, *Nicomachean Ethics*, 367.

95. Ibid., 368.

96. Arendt, *The Human Condition*, 49.

97. Virno, *A Grammar of the Multitude*, 55.

98. Ibid., 56.

99. Ibid., 63.

100. Ibid., 64–65.

101. Ibid., 66.

102. Available at http://www.elec.qmul.ac.uk/researchopenday/.

103. Alex McLean, *feedback.pl* (2004), cited in "Hacking Perl in Nightclubs," *Perl.com*. Available at http://www.perl.com/pub/2004/08/31/livecode.html.

104. Alex McLean, quoted in Robert Andrews, "Real DJs Code Live," *Wired*, 7 March 2006; available at http://www.wired.com/science/discoveries/news/2006/07/71248.

105. Adrian Mackenzie, *Cutting Code: Software and Sociality* (New York: Peter Lang, 2006), 141.

106. Ibid., 178.

107. radioqualia (Adam Hyde and Honor Harger), *Free Radio Linux* (2001); see http://www.radioqualia.net/documentation/frl/index.html.

108. Simon Yuill, "All Problems of Notation Will Be Solved by the Masses," *Mute* (February 2008); available at http://www.metamute.org/en/All-Problems-of-Notation-Will-be-Solved-by-the-Masses.

109. Virno, *A Grammar of the Multitude*, 90.

110. In Christian Marazzi, *Capital and Language: From the New Economy to the War Economy*, trans. Gregory Conti (Los Angeles: Semiotext(e), 2008), 156.

111. Ibid., 34.

112. Berardi, *The Soul at Work*, 22.

113. Ibid., 117–118. Berardi refers to this as the "psychopathology of desire," further developing Guattari's use of desire as a field of operation, open to capture by Disney or Microsoft as well as by social movements.

114. Ibid., 90.

115. Franco "Bifo" Berardi, *Precarious Rhapsody: Semiocapitalism and the Pathologies of the Post-Alpha Generation* (London: Minor Compositions, 2009), 43.

116. "Hong Kong Facebook 'Suicide' Group Investigated," *BBC News*, 26 November 2009; available at http://news.bbc.co.uk/2/hi/8380297.stm.

117. Berardi, *Precarious Rhapsody*, 55.

118. Jason Smith, "Preface: Soul on Strike," in Berardi, *The Soul at Work*, 19.

119. Aaron Koblin and Daniel Massey, *Bicycle Built for Two Thousand* (2009; available at http://www.bicyclebuiltfortwothousand.com/). The choice of the song "Daisy Bell" is explained on the site: "originally written by Harry Dacre in 1892, was made famous in 1962 by John Kelly, Max Mathews, and Carol Lockbaum as the first example of musical speech synthesis. In contrast to the 1962 version, *Bicycle Built for 2,000* was synthesized with a distributed system of human voices from all over the world."

120. *2001: A Space Odyssey* (1968, dir. Stanley Kubrick, Metro-Goldwyn-Mayer). HAL is a computer capable of speech, speech recognition, facial recognition, natural language processing, lip reading, art appreciation, interpreting and reproducing emotional behaviors, reasoning, and playing chess.

121. The full story was on the Forumwarz blog but is no longer available. See http://en.wikipedia.org/wiki/Forumwarz. Thanks to Robert Jackson for identifying this example.

122. Ibid.

123. Berardi, *The Soul at Work*, 89.

124. Ibid., 207.

125. This is something that Berardi also identifies in the article "An Introduction to Therapoetry: The Voice Against the Image / Poetry Against Semiocapital," in Geoff Cox, Nav Haq, and Tom Trevor, eds., "Art, Activism and Recuperation," *Concept Store Journal* 3 (Bristol: Arnolfini, 2010).

3   Coding Publics

1. Of particular relevance to the discussion in this chapter are Virno's *A Grammar of the Multitude* and Kelty's *Two Bits: the Cultural Significance of Free Software*. Both are cited and discussed further on.

2. Hannah Arendt, *The Human Condition* (1958; Chicago: University of Chicago Press, 1998), 23. She cites Aristotle to stress a definition of political action as distinct from the social, the latter being not a specifically human condition but more generally related to other animals. Some of this distinction is lost in translation from Greek to Latin, the terms "political" and "social" becoming confused and somewhat interchangeable according to Arendt.

3. Ibid., 176.

4. Paolo Virno, *A Grammar of the Multitude: For an Analysis of Contemporary Forms of Life*, trans. Isabella Bertoletti, James Cascaito, and Andrea Casson (New York: Semiotext(e), 2004), 51.

5. The phrase "Arab Spring" refers to the revolutionary wave of demonstrations and protests in the Arab world that began in Tunisia in December 2010 and have been noted for shared techniques of resistance, as well as the use of social media to organize. By spring of 2011, actions had spread to other countries including Algeria, Egypt, Yemen, and Libya. Examples of groups opposing cuts to public services include Uncut, a grassroots antiausterity action network, particularly in the UK and US (see http://www.ukuncut.org.uk/ and http://usuncut.org/).

6. See Cassell Bryan-Low and Siobhan Gorman, "Inside the Anonymous Army of 'Hacktivist' Attackers," *Wall Street Journal*, 23 June 2011; available at http://online.wsj.com/article/SB10001424052702304887904576399871831156018.html#ixzz1QJzHz74Y.

7. Formed in 2003, 4chan is a simple image-based bulletin board where anyone can post comments and share images (see http://www.4chan.org/).

8. See http://en.wikipedia.org/wiki/Anonymous_%28group%29. The documentary *Generation OS13: The New Culture of Resistance* (2011) charts the attack on civil liberties occurring in western democracies. Available at http://www.youtube.com/watch?feature=player_embedded&v=vY4VZr8Ox94#!

9. Occupy Wall Street was also inspired by the wave of other insurrectionary activities across the world, not least the Spanish Indignado movement. (See http://occupywallst.org/.)

10. The use of hashtags has become increasingly popular, reflecting the widespread use of Twitter as the medium of choice for political mobilization.

11. Organized through websites such as "Occupy Together." (See http://www.occupytogether.org/.)

12. Arendt, *The Human Condition*, 198.

13. Ibid., 38.

14. F.A.T./Aram Bartholl, *Occupy the Internet!* (2011). The publicity asks: "Are you interested in taking part in the recent global wave of revolution from the comfort of your home computer? Occupy the Internet!" (Available at http://fffff.at/occupy-the-internet/.)

15. Ibid. The website explains: "UPDATE (10-20-2011): Occupy Service! Force-occupy any website with 'Occupy The Internet—The Service'. Just insert a URL and send-out the link! fffff.at/occupy. Example: Goldmansachs.com occupied!!!" (Available at http://fffff.at/occupy/goldmansachs.com.)

16. Pall Thayer, *Protest* (2011; available at http://pallit.lhi.is/microcodes/contr.php?code_id =66).

17. See, for instance, the intervention at the Panel for Education Policy in New York, 26 October 2011, http://www.youtube.com/watch?v=YbmjMickJMA.

18. Nick Couldry, *Why Voice Matters: Culture and Politics after Neoliberalism* (London: Sage, 2010), 3.

19. Arendt, *The Human Condition*, 40.

20. Jon B. Alterman, "The Revolution Will Not Be Tweeted," *Washington Quarterly* 34 (4) (2011): 103–104; available at http://www.twq.com/11autumn/docs/11autumn_Alterman.pdf.

21. Bob Garfield, "Simon Cowell's Twitter Revolution," *Guardian*, 26 October 2011; available at http://www.guardian.co.uk/commentisfree/cifamerica/2011/oct/26/simon-cowell-twitter -revolution.

22. Ibid.

23. The Museum of Ordure is an artist project first founded by Stuart Brisley, Geoff Cox, and Adrian Ward in 2001. Although using the multiple name Rosse Yael Sirb as Acting Director, its current members are Maya Balgioglu, Stuart Brisley, Geoff Cox, and Les Liens Invisibles. (See http://www.ordure.org.)

24. Its first website, released under the institutional name "The UK Museum of Ordure," including the following curatorial statement: "Everything that is represented in the Museum of Ordure is subject to the vagaries of an uncontrolled internal process which slowly deforms and disables all information held in the museum. This is comparable to the decaying processes which affect all artifacts in museums, regardless of all attempts at preservation: the retouching, repainting, cleaning, etc, which are incorporated risks to the purity of artifacts when first acquired by museums. Even 'successful' renovations are subject to periodic changes resulting from shifts in conservation policies. Eventually (and in accordance with the fallibility of memory) artifacts are institutionally, progressively, determinedly and inadvertently altered by acts of conservation (sometimes unintentional acts of institutional vandalism) until they cease to be recognizable as the objects first acquired. Of course in both cases—in the virtual environment and in the material world—the processes of generation, decay, and entropy are paramount. Museums are by this definition charged with achieving the impossible." (Available at http://www.museum-ordure .org.uk/About_the_Museum/.)

25. It should be clear that this is rather different from what is understood as "garbage collection" in computer science, a term applied to the attempt to reclaim memory occupied by objects that are no longer in use by the program. It refers to automatic memory management, a term invented by John McCarthy around 1959 to solve problems in Lisp. (See http://en.wikipedia.org/wiki/ Garbage_collection_%28computer_science%29.)

26. The account is now suspended; see http://twitter.com/#!/MuseumOfOrdure. A real-time simulation is available at http://www.ordure.org/mootwitter.

27. Georges Bataille, *The Accursed Share*, trans. Robert Hurley (New York: Zone Books, 1988–1991). The production of nonutilitarian or luxury goods related to waste, sacrifice, or destruction is able to escape the imperatives of capitalism.

28. Available at http://www.ordure.org.

29. Dominque Laporte, *History of Shit* (1978; Cambridge, MA: MIT Press, 2000), 7. This is a reference to Paul Éluard's *Capitale de la douleur*.

30. Ibid., 18.

31. Karl Marx, *Grundrisse: Foundations of the Critique of Political Economy (Rough Draft)* (Harmondsworth: Penguin, 1981), 273.

32. See Gethin Chamberlain, "Apple's Chinese Workers Treated Inhumanely, Like Machines," *Guardian*, 5 May 2011; available at http://www.guardian.co.uk/technology/2011/apr/30/apple -chinese-workers-treated-inhumanely. The article claims that more than half a million Chinese workers are paid around 65p an hour, working over 60 hours a week to cope with the massive demand.

33. For instance, enormous amounts of exported e-waste ends up in Guiyu, China, a recycling hub with the highest level of cancer-causing dioxins in the world. See Bryan Walsh, "E-Waste Not," Time.com, 8 January 2009; available at http://www.time.com/time/magazine/article/ 0,9171,1870485,00.html#ixzz1HMrhkfVP.

34. As Roberto Saviano confirms: "Waste grounds are the most concrete emblems of every economic cycle." In *Gomorrah* (2006), cited in Franco "Bifo" Berardi, *Precarious Rhapsody: Semiocapitalism and the Pathologies of the Post-Alpha Generation* (London: Minor Compositions, 2009), 53.

35. Laporte, *History of Shit*, 10.

36. James Boyle, "Fencing Off Ideas: Enclosure and the Disappearance of the Public Domain," in Rishab Aiyer Ghosh, ed., *Code: Collaborative Ownership and the Digital Economy* (Cambridge, MA: MIT Press, 2005), 237.

37. Michael Hardt and Antonio Negri, *Commonwealth* (Cambridge, MA: Harvard University Press, 2009).

38. James Leach, "Modes of Creativity and the Register of Ownership," in Ghosh, *Code*.

39. Ibid., 33–34.

40. Ibid., 35.

41. GNU General Public License; available at http://www.gnu.org/copyleft/gpl.html.

42. Leach, "Modes of Creativity and the Register of Ownership," 41.

43. Yochai Benkler, "Coase's Penguin, or, Linux and the Nature of the Firm," in Ghosh, *Code*, 169. He is referring to the economist Ronald Coase's essay "The Nature of the Firm," of 1937.

44. Michel Bauwens, "The Social Web and Its Social Contracts: Some Notes on Social Antagonism in Netarchical Capitalism," *Re-Public* (2008; available at http://www.re-public.gr/en/?p=261).

45. Ibid.

46. Ibid.

47. Virno, *A Grammar of the Multitude*, 110.

48. Christopher M. Kelty, *Two Bits: The Cultural Significance of Free Software* (Durham: Duke University Press, 2008), 143–178.

49. Ibid., 113.

50. Richard M. Stallman, *Free Software, Free Society: Selected Essays of Richard M. Stallman*, ed. Joshua Gay (Boston: GNU Press, 2002), 41. The phrase is further explored by Superflex in their project *Free Beer*, as they playfully collapse the distinction: "FREE BEER is a beer which is free in the sense of freedom, not in the sense of free beer" (available at http://www.superflex.net/projects/freebeer/). Also see Stian Rødven Eide, ed., *Free Beer 1.0* (Göteborg: FSCONS, 2009).

51. Stallman, *Free Software, Free Society*, 15.

52. The freedoms read like commandments: "Freedom 0: The freedom to run the program, for any purpose; Freedom 1: The freedom to study how the program works, and adapt it to your needs. (Access to the source code is a precondition for this.); Freedom 2: The freedom to redistribute copies so you can help your neighbor; Freedom 3: The freedom to improve the program, and release your improvements to the public, so that the whole community benefits. (Access to the source code is a precondition for this.)" Ibid., 41.

53. Gabriella Coleman, "Code Is Speech: Legal Tinkering, Expertise, and Protest among Free and Open Source Software Developers," *Cultural Anthropology* 24 (3) (2009): 433–434; available at http://gabriellacoleman.org/.

54. The Universal Declaration of Human Rights (adopted in 1948); available at http://www.un.org/en/documents/udhr/.

55. The European Convention on Human Rights (adopted in 1950); available at http://www.hri.org/docs/ECHR50.html.

56. Established by an Act of Parliament in 1872, Speakers' Corner is an area where public speaking is allowed, and is located in the northeast corner of Hyde Park, London. This persists as a legacy of allowing the free "last words" of the condemned at the site of public execution, at nearby Tyburn. (See http://www.speakerscorner.net/articles/tyburnhangingtreeandtheoriginsofspeakerscorner.) Embracing the notion of free speech on the Internet, the website SpeakersCorner contained articles (such as the one mentioned above), videos, and an online radio show (available at http://www.speakerscorner.net/).

57. The Electronic Frontier Foundation (EFF) is an organization dedicated to protecting freedom of speech on the Internet. See http://www.eff.org/.

58. A summary of WikiLeaks is available at http://wikileaks.org/About.html.

59. Key to this project were the ten Macy conferences held between 1946 and 1953, which developed ideas around informational systems and a universal theory of regulation and control that would be applicable to humans as well as to machines, to economic systems as well as to behavior. See http://en.wikipedia.org/wiki/Macy_conferences.

60. David M. Berry, *Copy, Rip, Burn: The Politics of Copyleft and Open Source* (London: Pluto Press, 2008), 182.

61. Ibid., 185.

62. Ibid., 192.

63. Ibid., 199.

64. Ibid., 79.

65. See Bruno Latour, *Reassembling the Social: An Introduction to Actor-Network-Theory* (Oxford: Oxford University Press, 2005). Indeed, a number of terms in popular usage require closer description, especially if the intention is to begin to explore new formations that are able to perform

collective functions. The use of the term "social," among many others, has become so common-place that it seems emptied of meaning.

66. Ibid., 22. The uncertainty principle states that certain pairs of physical properties cannot be known beyond a specified level of precision at the same time. See http://en.wikipedia.org/wiki/Uncertainty_principle.

67. Christophe Bruno, *Human Browser* (2005; available at http://www.iterature.com/human-browser/en/).

68. Latour, *Reassembling the Social*, 59.

69. Albert-László Barabási, *Linked: The New Science of Networks* (Cambridge, MA: Perseus, 2002), 80.

70. Ibid., 66.

71. Ibid., 86.

72. DARPA's motivation was to develop a robust communications infrastructure for use by its projects at universities and research laboratories in the US, but whether it was developed to withstand attack from a nuclear strike, feared at the time of the Cold War, is rather more contentious. See http://en.wikipedia.org/wiki/ARPANET.

73. Ibid. The Advanced Research Projects Agency Network (ARPANET), initially known as ARPA (1963), was the world's first operational packet-switching network. The first message ever sent via the ARPANET was at 10:30 PM, October 29, 1969.

74. Alex Galloway, *Protocol: How Control Exists after Decentralization* (Cambridge, MA: MIT Press, 2004), 7.

75. Ibid.

76. Richard Wray, "EU Says Internet Could Fall Apart," *Guardian*, 12 October 2005; available at http://www.guardian.co.uk/business/2005/oct/12/newmedia.media.

77. Ned Rossiter, *Organized Networks: Media Theory, Creative Labour, New Institutions* (Rotterdam: NAi, in association with the Institute of Network Cultures, 2006).

78. Rui Guerra/INTK, *www_hack* (2008–2010; available at http://www.intk.com/www_hack/). Aram Bartholl's *Occupy the Internet!* (2011; available at http://fffff.at/occupy-the-internet/), mentioned earlier in the chapter, uses the same technical solution of embedding JavaScript in the html page.

79. See http://libreplanet.org/wiki/Group:NoJavaScript.

80. Rossiter, *Organized Networks*, 36.

81. Carl Schmitt, *The Concept of the Political* (1927; Chicago: University of Chicago Press, 1996).

82. Jacques Rancière, "Ten Theses on Politics," *Theory and Event* 5 (3) (2001). That the term democracy contains *demos* (the people) and *kratein* (to rule) is further reflected in Rancière's call for a rupturing of the very "axioms of democracy" (of ruling and being ruled). Available at http://muse.jhu.edu/journals/theory_and_event/v005/5.3ranciere.html.

83. Rossiter, *Organized Networks*, 39.

84. *The Social Network* (2010; available at http://www.thesocialnetwork-movie.com).

85. Alexander R. Galloway and Eugene Thacker, *The Exploit: A Theory of Networks* (Minneapolis: University of Minnesota Press, 2007).

86. Walter Benjamin, "Critique of Violence" (1921), in *Walter Benjamin: Selected Writings*, vol. 1, *1913–1926*, ed. Marcus Bullock and Michael W. Jennings (Cambridge, MA: Harvard University Press, 1996), 243.

87. Giorgio Agamben, *State of Exception*, trans. Kevin Attell (Chicago: University of Chicago Press, 2005). The reference to Schmitt is from his "Politische Theologie" of 1922.

88. Ibid., 4.

89. Shiv Malik, "Facebook Accused of Removing Activists' Pages," *Guardian*, 29 April 2011; available at http://www.guardian.co.uk/technology/2011/apr/29/facebook-accused-removing-activists -pages. Also see note 105 for another example.

90. "Facebook's New Terms of Service: 'We Can Do Anything We Want with Your Content. Forever.'" Posted on consumerist.com and cited in Jessica E. Vascellaro, "Facebook's About-Face on Data," *Wall Street Journal*, 19 February 2009; available at http://online.wsj.com/article/ SB123494484088908625.html#ixzz1dCjqZGSk. Facebook's Terms of Service are available at http://www.facebook.com/legal/terms.

91. Bauwens, "The Social Web and Its Social Contracts."

92. See Thomas H. Davenport and John C. Beck, *The Attention Economy: Understanding the New Economy of Business* (Boston: Harvard Business School Press, 2001).

93. The figures are taken from the *Financial Times*, 6 January 2011, and from Facebook's publicity material. Both are quoted in Adam Avidsson and Elanor Colleoni, "Value in Informational Capitalism and on the Internet: A Reply to Christian Fuchs," *Social Science Research Network*, 28 February 2011; available at http://papers.ssrn.com/sol3/papers.cfm?abstract_id=1772975.

94. Bauwens, "The Social Web and Its Social Contracts."

95. Maurizio Lazzarato, "Immaterial Labor," in Paolo Virno and Michael Hardt, eds., *Radical Thought in Italy: A Potential Politics* (Minneapolis: University of Minnesota Press, 1996), 142.

96. See the chapter "Soft Control" in Tiziana Terranova, *Network Culture: Politics for the Information Age* (London: Pluto Press, 2004), 98–130.

97. Moddr_, *Web2.0 Suicide Machine* (2009; available at http://suicidemachine.org).

98. Les Liens Invisibles, *Seppukoo* (2009; available at http://www.seppukoo.com/.)

99. Thanks to Tatiana Bazzichelli for pointing out these connections. For more on the multiple identity Luther Blissett, initiated in 1994, see http://www.lutherblissett.net/.

100. Loretta Borrelli, "The Suicide Irony: Seppukoo and Web 2.0 Suicide Machine," *Digimag* 52 (March 2010; available at http://www.digicult.it/digimag/article.asp?id=1733). *Tiqqun* is the name of a French journal launched in 1999, closely associated with the squatting and autonomist movements as well as the situationist and anarchist traditions. For more on the group Tiqqun, see their *This Is Not a Program* (Los Angeles: Semiotext(e), 2011).

101. Paolo Cirio and Alessandro Ludovico, *Face to Facebook* (2011; available at http://www .face-to-facebook.net). Extensive documentation and media reaction are available online. The project forms part of what the artists refer to as their *Monopolism Trilogy*, expropriating the holy trinity of Google, Amazon, and Facebook. The earlier works were produced in collaboration with UBERMORGEN.com: *Google Will Eat Itself* (2005; available at http://www.gwei.org/index.php) and *Amazon Noir* (2006; available at http://www.amazon-noir.com/). UBERMORGEN.com produced their own *EKMRZ_trilogy*, with the project *The Sound of Ebay* (2009; available at http:// www.sound-of-ebay.com/100.php) as the final installment.

102. Available at http://www.lovely-faces.com/.

103. Jodi Dean, *Democracy and Other Neoliberal Fantasies: Communicative Capitalism and Left Politics* (Durham: Duke University Press, 2009), 49.

104. Les Liens Invisibles, *Repetitionr.com* (2010), commissioned by Arnolfini; available at http://www.repetitionr.com/.

105. iPetitions, for instance, was used to respond to fifty-one profiles operated by UK anti-cuts groups, political organizations, and activist campaigns being suspended or deleted by Facebook (29 April 2011). Available at http://www.ipetitions.com/petition/deletion-of-activist-facebook-profiles/.

106. Overidentification is a tactic often associated with Žižek, as well as groups like The Yes Men or provocateurs such as Laibach. It is used to expose a position by pushing the system to its extremes in order to show that it is unacceptable.

107. Les Liens Invisibles, *Tweet4Action.com* (2011), commissioned by Turbulence; available at http://turbulence.org/works/tweet4action/. It should be added that despite the line of argument here, initiatives like "speak4tweet" perform a useful service, but it addresses what is already a conceptual paradox. The recent example of a Facebook page proposed against censorship on Facebook follows a similar paradoxical logic. (Available at http://www.facebook.com/group.php?gid=42420648943.)

108. UBERMORGEN.com, *[V]ote-Auction* (2000; available at http://www.vote-auction.net).

109. The project is well documented online (ibid.). The inconsistencies include that the DNS registrar in Switzerland shut down all services on the domain without notice, despite being outside US jurisdiction. For more reactions, see also "Burden of Proof," *CNN* (2000), 27-minute video feature (available at http://www.vote-auction.net/movies/CNN_Burdenofproof_360x288.html).

110. UBERMORGEN.com, *The Injunction Generator* (2003; available at http://ipnic.org/intro.html).

111. Dean, *Democracy and Other Neoliberal Fantasies*, 52.

112. Michel Foucault, *The Government of Self and Others: Lectures at the Collège de France 1982–1983* (Basingstoke: Palgrave Macmillan, 2010).

113. For example, the P2P virtual currency Bitcoin created in 2009 replaces the centralized bank with the distributed network, thus offering a critique of monopolistic practices. (See http://www.bitcoin.org/.)

114. Despite being written as a joke, it brought the attention of the FBI, and Kamkar pled guilty to a felony charge of computer hacking, agreeing not to use a computer for three years. Further explanations and press coverage of the Sam Kamkar case are available at http://namb.la/popular/.

115. Couldry, *Why Voice Matters*, 10, 11.

116. Berardi, *Precarious Rhapsody*, 72.

117. Coleman, "Code Is Speech," 422.

118. Kelty, *Two Bits*, 27–63.

119. Ibid., 3.

120. Ibid., 58.

121. Etienne Balibar, *Spinoza and Politics*, trans. Peter Snowdon (1998; London: Verso, 2008), 25.

122. Ibid., 27.

123. Ibid., 30.

124. Ibid., 31.

125. Ibid. 114.

126. Ibid., 116.

127. Couldry, *Why Voice Matters*, 73.

128. Boris Groys, *The Communist Postscript* (London: Verso, 2009), xvii.

129. Ibid., 4.

130. Ibid., 8.

131. Kelty, *Two Bits*, 116.

132. Berardi, *Precarious Rhapsody*, 60. He is invoking general intellect or networked intelligence, discussed at length in the previous chapter, in particular through the work of Virno, and is building upon Antonio Gramsci's concept of the "organic intellectual."

4   Code for-Itself

1. Hannah Arendt, *The Human Condition* (1958; Chicago: University of Chicago Press, 1998), 5.

2. Ibid., 4.

3. Franco "Bifo" Berardi, *Precarious Rhapsody: Semiocapitalism and the Pathologies of the Post-Alpha Generation* (London: Minor Compositions, 2009), 9. He is quoting Rose Golden from 1975.

4. N. Katherine Hayles, *My Mother Was a Computer* (Chicago: University of Chicago Press, 2005), 1.

5. John Armitage, "From Discourse Networks to Cultural Mathematics: An Interview with Friedrich A. Kittler," *Theory, Culture and Society* 23 (17) (2006): 19. Kittler's *Discourse Networks, 1800/1900* is about discourses of institutional power, drawing on the discourse analysis of Foucault but also on Weaver and Shannon's information theory (1949). I am also aware that there is a danger of perpetuating gender stereotypes here, as clearly the mother is not necessarily charged with the task of learning reading.

6. Hayles, *My Mother Was a Computer*, 17–30.

7. Judith Butler, *Excitable Speech: A Politics of the Performative* (London: Routledge, 1997), 1.

8. Slavoj Žižek, *Violence* (London: Profile Books, 2008), 52, 58. He also refers to the hegemonic operations of language in the work of Laclau and the ontological violence of language in Heidegger.

9. Walter Benjamin, "Critique of Violence" (1921), in *Walter Benjamin: Selected Writings*, vol. 1, *1913–1926*, ed. Marcus Bullock and Michael W. Jennings (Cambridge, Mass.: Harvard University Press, 1996), 236–252.

10. Žižek, *Violence*, 168.

11. SQL injection techniques exploit security vulnerability occurring in the database layer of an application (like queries).

12. Some ideas related to this were developed by Geoff Cox and Martin Knahl in "Critique of Software Security," in Geoff Cox and Wolfgang Sützl, eds., *Creating Insecurity* (New York: Autonomedia, 2009), 27–43.

13. After 50 days of hacks against governments, institutions, and corporations, LulzSec announced it was time to disappear (on 26 June 2011); available at http://pastebin.com/1znEGmHa.

14. Paolo Virno, *Multitude: Between Innovation and Negation*, trans. Isabella Bertoletti, James Cascaito, and Andrea Casson (Los Angeles: Semiotext(e), 2008), 19. He is referring to Aristotle's *Ethics*.

15. Ibid., 20.

16. Ibid., 69.

17. Ibid., 72.

18. Ibid., 73, 74.

19. Ibid. 165.

20. Ibid., 82, 83.

21. Ibid., 46, 47.

22. Ibid., 24.

23. It is worth clarifying that a determinate negation in mathematics is not simply negative, and there are many examples of nothing as art, such as John Cage's *4'33"* (1952), somewhat explained by the statement, "Every something is an echo of Nothing," in *Silence: Lectures and Writings* (Middletown, CT: Wesleyan University Press, 1961), 131.

24. Slavoj Žižek, *The Ticklish Subject: The Absent Centre of Political Ontology* (London: Verso, 1999), 72. He is explaining the gap that separates the negated system's "real" death from its "symbolic" death.

25. Virno, *Multitude*, 63.

26. Ibid., 50.

27. Butler, *Excitable Speech*, 15.

28. Virno, *Multitude*, 50.

29. Žižek, *The Ticklish Subject*, 18.

30. Ibid., 60. Further invoked here is the input-output automaton *Canard Digérateur*, or *Digesting Duck*, created by Jacques de Vaucanson in 1739, which appeared to eat grain, metabolize, and defecate. A replica of Vaucanson's mechanical duck, created by Frédéric Vidoni, can be seen at the Musée des Automates, Grenoble, France.

31. Virno, *Multitude*, 190.

32. The slogan "Information wants to be free" is attributed to Stewart Brand, who argued that technology could be liberating rather than oppressing. The earliest recorded occurrence of the expression was at the first Hackers Conference in 1984. Brand said: "On the one hand information wants to be expensive, because it's so valuable. The right information in the right place just changes your life. On the other hand, information wants to be free, because the cost of getting it out is getting lower and lower all the time. So you have these two fighting against each other." Available at http://en.wikipedia.org/wiki/Information_wants_to_be_free.

33. See Thomas H. Davenport and John C. Beck, *The Attention Economy: Understanding the New Economy of Business* (Boston: Harvard Business School Press, 2001).

34. Berardi, *Precarious Rhapsody*, 113.

35. Ibid., 54.

36. Available at http://www.digitalcraft.org/iloveyou/loveletter_reading.htm. The virus source code is available at http://www.cexx.org/loveletter.htm.

37. The virus also inspired the exhibition "I Love You [rev.eng]," curated by digitalcraft.org/ Franziska Nori in 2002, at the Museum für angewandte Kunst in Frankfurt am Main. (See http://www.digitalcraft.org/iloveyou/index.htm.) A further example of a virus as artwork is the *biennale.py* virus that contaminated the Venice Biennale's website in 2000, produced by 0100101110101101.org with epidemiC for the Slovenian pavilion. (See http://www.0100101110101101.org/home/biennale_py/.)

38. David Link, "There Must Be an Angel: On the Beginnings of the Arithmetics of Rays," in Siegfried Zielinski and David Link, eds., *Variantology 2: On Deep Time Relations of Arts, Sciences and Technologies* (Cologne: König, 2006), 15–42; available at http://www.alpha60.de/research/ muc/.

39. Ibid.

40. Ibid. Interestingly, Link's essay makes reference to Hegel's dialectics of essence and appearance.

41. Ibid.

42. David Link, "Scrambling T-R-U-T-H: Rotating Letters as a Material Form of Thought," in Siegfried Zielinski and Eckhard Fürlus, eds., *Variantology 4: On Deep Time Relations of Arts, Sciences and Technologies in the Arabic-Islamic World* (Cologne: König, 2010), 215–266.

43. Mladen Dolar, *A Voice and Nothing More* (Cambridge, MA: MIT Press, 2006), 106.

44. Giorgio Agamben, *Homo Sacer: Sovereign Power and Bare Life*, trans. Daniel Heller-Roazen (Stanford: Stanford University Press, 1998), 26–27.

45. Dolar, *A Voice and Nothing More*, 9. A fuller description of this line of argument stands in chapter 2.

References

Adorno, Theodor. *Minima Moralia: Reflections from Damaged Life*. Trans. E. F. N. Jephcott. London: Verso, 1978.

Agamben, Giorgio. *Homo Sacer: Sovereign Power and Bare Life*. Trans. Daniel Heller-Roazen. Stanford: Stanford University Press, 1998.

Agamben, Giorgio. *Means without Ends: Notes on Politics*. Trans. Vincenzo Binetti and Cesare Casarino. Minneapolis: University of Minnesota Press, 2000.

Agamben, Giorgio. *State of Exception*. Trans. Kevin Attell. Chicago: University of Chicago Press, 2005.

Alterman, Jon B. "The Revolution Will Not Be Tweeted." *Washington Quarterly* 34 (4) (2011): 103–116. Available at http://www.twq.com/11autumn/docs/11autumn_Alterman.pdf.

Althusser, Louis. "Ideology and Ideological State Apparatuses: Notes Toward an Investigation." In Slavoj Zizek, ed., *Mapping Ideology*, 100–140. London: Verso, 1997.

Andrews, Robert. "Real DJs Code Live." *Wired*, 7 March 2006. Available at http://www.wired.com/science/discoveries/news/2006/07/71248.

Archer, Margaret, Roy Bhaskar, Andrew Collier, Tony Lawson, and Alan Norrie, eds. *Critical Realism: Essential Readings*. London: Routledge, 1998.

Arendt, Hannah. *The Human Condition*. 1958; Chicago: University of Chicago Press, 1998.

Arendt, Hannah. "Labor, Work, Action" (1964). In *The Portable Hannah Arendt*, 167–181. New York: Penguin, 2000.

Aristotle. *Nicomachean Ethics* (325 BC). In John Cottingham, ed. and trans., *Western Philosophy: An Anthology*, 326–370. Oxford: Blackwell, 1996.

Aristotle. *On the Soul and On Memory and Recollection*. Trans. Joe Sachs. Santa Fe: Green Lion Press, 2001.

Armitage, John. "From Discourse Networks to Cultural Mathematics: An Interview with Friedrich A. Kittler." *Theory, Culture and Society* 23 (17) (2006). Available at http://tcs.sagepub.com/content/23/7-8/17.

Arns, Inke. "Read_Me, Run_Me, Execute_Me: Software and Its Discontents, or, It's the Performativity of Code, Stupid." In Olga Goriunova and Alexei Shulgin, eds., *Read_Me: Software Art and Cultures*, 176–193. Aarhus: Digital Aesthetics Research Centre, University of Aarhus, 2004.

Austin, J. L. *How to Do Things with Words*. Cambridge, MA: Harvard University Press, 1975.

Avidsson, Adam, and Elanor Colleoni. "Value in Informational Capitalism and on the Internet: A Reply to Christian Fuchs." *Social Science Research Network* (28 February 2011). Available at http://papers.ssrn.com/sol3/papers.cfm?abstract_id=1772975.

Badiou, Alain. *Number and Numbers*. Cambridge: Polity Press, 2008.

Bakhtin, Mikhail. *The Dialogic Imagination: Four Essays*. Ed. Michael Holquist. Austin: University of Texas Press, 1981.

Balibar, Etienne. *Spinoza and Politics*. Trans. Peter Snowdon. 1998; London: Verso, 2008.

Barabási, Albert-László. *Linked: The New Science of Networks*. Cambridge, MA: Perseus, 2002.

Barthes, Roland. *Image, Music, Text*. London: Fontana, 1977.

Barthes, Roland. *S/Z: An Essay*. London: Cape, 1974.

Bataille, Georges. *The Accursed Share*. 3 vols. in 2. Trans. Robert Hurley. New York: Zone Books, 1988–1991.

Bateson, Gregory. *Mind and Nature: A Necessary Unity*. Cresskill, NJ: Hampton Press, 1979.

Bateson, Gregory. *Steps to an Ecology of Mind*. 1971; Chicago: University of Chicago Press, 2000.

Bauwens, Michel. "The Social Web and Its Social Contracts: Some Notes on Social Antagonism in Netarchical Capitalism." *Re-Public* (2008). Available at http://www.re-public.gr/en/?p=261.

Benjamin, Walter. "Critique of Violence." In *Selected Writings*, vol. 1, *1913–1926*. Ed. Marcus Bullock and Michael W. Jennings. Cambridge, MA: Belknap Press, 1996.

Benjamin, Walter. "On the Concept of History." In *Selected Writings*, vol. 4, *1938–1940*. Ed. Howard Eiland and Michael W. Jennings. Cambridge, MA: Belknap Press, 2003.

Bense, Max. "The Projects of Generative Aesthetics." In Jasia Reichardt, ed., *Cybernetics, Art, and Ideas*. London: Studio Vista, 1971. Available at http://www.computerkunst.org/Bense_Manifest.pdf.

Berardi, Franco "Bifo." *Precarious Rhapsody: Semiocapitalism and the Pathologies of the Post-Alpha Generation*. London: Minor Compositions, 2009.

Berardi, Franco "Bifo." *The Soul at Work: From Alienation to Autonomy*. Trans. Francesca Cadel and Giuseppina Mecchia. Los Angeles: Semiotext(e), 2009.

Berry, David M. *Copy, Rip, Burn: The Politics of Copyleft and Open Source*. London: Pluto Press, 2008.

Bogost, Ian. *Persuasive Games: The Expressive Power of Videogames*. Cambridge, MA: MIT Press, 2007.

Bogost, Ian. *Unit Operations: An Approach to Videogame Criticism*. Cambridge, MA: MIT Press, 2004.

Bolter, Jay David. *Turing's Man: Western Culture in the Computer Age*. Chapel Hill: University of North Carolina Press, 1984.

Bolter, Jay, and Richard Grusin. *Remediation: Understanding New Media*. Cambridge, MA: MIT Press, 1999.

Borrelli, Loretta. "The Suicide Irony: Seppukoo and Web 2.0 Suicide Machine." *Digimag* 52 (March 2010). Available at http://www.digicult.it/digimag/article.asp?id=1733.

Bosma, Josephine, et al., eds. *Readme! Filtered by Nettime: ASCII Culture and the Revenge of Knowledge*. New York: Autonomedia, 1999.

Bryan-Low, Cassell, and Siobhan Gorman. "Inside the Anonymous Army of 'Hacktivist' Attackers." *Wall Street Journal*, 23 June 2011. Available at http://online.wsj.com/article/SB10001424052702304887904576399871831156018.html#ixzz1QJzHz74Y.

Butler, Judith. *Excitable Speech: A Politics of the Performative*. London: Routledge, 1997.

Calvino, Italo. "How I Wrote One of My Books." In *Oulipo Laboratory*, trans. Iain White. London: Atlas, 1995.

Chamberlain, Gethin. "Apple's Chinese Workers Treated Inhumanely, Like Machines." *Guardian*, 5 May 2011. Available at http://www.guardian.co.uk/technology/2011/apr/30/apple-chinese -workers-treated-inhumanely.

Chomsky, Noam. *Syntactic Structures*. 1957; The Hague: Mouton, 1972.

Chun, Wendy Hui Kyong. "The Enduring Ephemeral, or the Future Is a Memory." *Critical Inquiry* 35 (1) (2008): 148–171.

Chun, Wendy Hui Kyong. "On 'Sourcery,' or Code as Fetish." *Configurations* 16 (3) (Fall 2008): 299–324.

Chun, Wendy Hui Kyong. *Programmed Visions: Software and Memory*. Cambridge, MA: MIT Press, 2011.

Cienki, Alan. "Why Study Metaphor and Gesture?" In Alan Cienki and Cornelia Müller, eds., *Metaphor and Gesture*, 5–25. Amsterdam: John Benjamins, 2008. Available at http:// benjamins.com/cgi-bin/t_bookview.cgi?bookid=GS%203.

Coleman, Gabriella. "Code Is Speech: Legal Tinkering, Expertise, and Protest among Free and Open Source Software Developers." *Cultural Anthropology* 24 (3) (2009): 420–454. Available at http://gabriellacoleman.org/.

Collins, Nick, Alex McLean, Julian Rohrhuber, and Adrian Ward. "Live Coding in Laptop Performance." *Organised Sound* 8 (3) (2003): 321–329.

Couldry, Nick. *Why Voice Matters: Culture and Politics after Neoliberalism*. London: Sage, 2010.

Cox, Geoff. *Antithesis: The Dialectics of Software Art*. Aarhus: Digital Aesthetic Research Centre, Aarhus University, 2010.

Cox, Geoff. "Means-End of Software." In Christian Ulrik Andersen and Søren Bro Pold, eds., *Interface Criticism: Aesthetics beyond Buttons*, 145–161. Aarhus: Aarhus University Press, 2011.

Cox, Geoff, Alex McLean, and Adrian Ward. "The Aesthetics of Generative Code." Paper delivered at Generative Art 00, international conference, Politecnico di Milano, Italy (2000). Available at http://www.generative.net/papers/aesthetics/index.html.

Cox, Geoff, Alex McLean, and Adrian Ward. "Coding Praxis: Reconsidering the Aesthetics of Code." In Olga Goriunova and Alexei Shulgin, eds., *Read_Me: Software Art and Cultures*, 161–174. Aarhus: Digital Aesthetics Research Centre, University of Aarhus, 2004.

Cox, Geoff, Haq Nav, and Tom Trevor, eds. "Art, Activism and Recuperation." *Concept Store Journal* 3. Bristol: Arnolfini, 2010.

Cox, Geoff, and Wolfgang Sützl, eds. *Creating Insecurity*. New York: Autonomedia, 2009.

Cramer, Florian. "Concepts, Notations, Software Art." In Olga Goriunova and Alexei Shulgin, eds., *Software Art: Thoughts*. Catalog of Read_Me Festival 1.2. Moscow: Rosizo, State Centre for Museums and Exhibitions, 2002.

Cramer, Florian. "Exe.cut[up]able statements: The Insistence of Code." In Gerfried Stocker and Christine Schöpf, eds., *Code: The Language of Our Time*. Linz: Ars Electronica; Ostfildern-Ruit: Hatje Cantz, 2003.

Cramer, Florian. *Words Made Flesh: Code, Culture, Imagination*. Rotterdam: Piet Zwart Institute, 2005. Available at http://www.netzliteratur.net/cramer/wordsmadefleshpdf.pdf.

Davenport, Thomas H., and John C. Beck. *The Attention Economy: Understanding the New Economy of Business*. Boston: Harvard Business School Press, 2001.

Dean, Jodi. *Democracy and Other Neoliberal Fantasies: Communicative Capitalism and Left Politics*. Durham: Duke University Press, 2009.

Dolar, Mladen. *A Voice and Nothing More*. Cambridge, MA: MIT Press, 2006.

Dourish, Paul. *Where the Action Is: The Foundations of Embodied Interaction*. Cambridge, MA: MIT Press, 2001.

Eide, Stian Rødven, ed. *Free Beer 1.0*. Göteborg: FSCONS, 2009.

Felderer, Brigitte. "Orality." In *Zauberhafte Klangmaschinen: Von der Sprechmaschine bis zur Sound-karte*. Hainburg: IMA Institut für Medienarchäologie, Schott Music, 2008.

Feuerstein, Steven. *Oracle PL/SQL Programming*. Cambridge, MA: O'Reilly, 1997.

Foerster, Heinz von. *Cybernetics of Cybernetics*. Urbana: University of Illinois, 1974.

Foucault, Michel. *The Government of Self and Others: Lectures at the Collège de France 1982–1983*. Basingstoke: Palgrave Macmillan, 2010.

Fuller, Matthew. *Behind the Blip: Essays on the Culture of Software*. New York: Autonomedia, 2003.

Fuller, Matthew. *Media Ecologies: Materialist Energies in Art and Technoculture*. Cambridge, MA: MIT Press, 2005.

Fuller, Matthew, ed. *Software Studies: A Lexicon*. Cambridge, MA: MIT Press, 2008.

Galloway, Alexander R. *Protocol: How Control Exists after Decentralization*. Cambridge, MA: MIT Press, 2004.

Galloway, Alexander R., and Eugene Thacker. *The Exploit: A Theory of Networks*. Minneapolis: University of Minnesota Press, 2007.

Garfield, Bob. "Simon Cowell's Twitter Revolution." *Guardian*, 26 October 2011. Available at http://www.guardian.co.uk/commentisfree/cifamerica/2011/oct/26/simon-cowell-twitter -revolution.

Ghosh, Rishab Aiyer, ed. *Code: Collaborative Ownership and the Digital Economy*. Cambridge, MA: MIT Press, 2005.

Giroux, Henry. *Living Dangerously: Multiculturalism and the Politics of Difference*. New York: Peter Lang, 1993.

Groys, Boris. *The Communist Postscript*. London: Verso, 2009.

Guattari, Félix. *Chaosophy*. Ed. Sylvère Lotringer. New York: Semiotext(e), 1995.

Hardt, Michael, and Antonio Negri. *Commonwealth*. Cambridge, MA: Harvard University Press, 2009.

Hardt, Michael, and Antonio Negri. *Empire*. Cambridge, MA: Harvard University Press, 2000.

Hawkes, Terence. *Structuralism and Semiotics*. 1977; London: Methuen, 1986.

Hayles, N. Katherine. *My Mother Was a Computer*. Chicago: University of Chicago Press, 2005.

Hayles, N. Katherine. *Writing Machines*. Cambridge, MA: MIT Press, 2002.

Hegel, Georg W. F. *The Phenomenology of Mind*. Trans. J. B. Baillie. New York: Harper and Row, 1967.

Hofstadter, Douglas R. *Gödel, Escher, Bach: An Eternal Golden Braid*. 1979; London: Penguin, 2000.

Holland, Owen, ed. *Machine Consciousness*. Exeter: Imprint Academic, 2003.

Holmes, Brian. "Artistic Autonomy and the Communication Society." In *Diffusion: Collaborative Practice in Contemporary Art*. London: Tate Modern, 2003.

hooks, bell. "Talking Back." In Russell Ferguson, Martha Gever, et al., eds., *Out There: Marginalization and Contemporary Cultures*. Cambridge, MA: MIT Press, 1989.

Jameson, Fredric. *The Prison-House of Language: A Critical Account of Structuralism and Russian Formalism*. Princeton: Princeton University Press, 1972.

Kelty, Christopher M. *Two Bits: The Cultural Significance of Free Software*. Durham: Duke University Press, 2008.

Kittler, Friedrich. *Discourse Networks 1800/1900*. Trans. M. Metteer and C. Cullens. Stanford: Stanford University Press, 1990.

Kittler, Friedrich. "Protected Mode." In Ute Bernhardt and Ingo Ruhmann, eds., *Computer, Macht und Gegenwehr. InformatikerInnen für eine andere Informatik*, 34–44. Bonn: FIfF, 1991.

Kittler, Friedrich. "There Is No Software." In Timothy Druckrey, ed., *Electronic Culture*, 331–337. New York: Aperture, 1996.

Kleiner, Dmytri. *The Telekommunist Manifesto*. Network Notebooks 03. Amsterdam: Institute of Network Cultures, 2010.

Knuth, Donald. *The Art of Computer Programming*. Vol. 1, *Fundamental Algorithms*. Reading, MA: Addison-Wesley, 1981.

Lakoff, George, and Mark Johnson. *Philosophy in the Flesh: The Embodied Mind and Its Challenge to Western Thought*. New York: HarperCollins, 1999.

Laporte, Dominique. *History of Shit*. Cambridge, MA: MIT Press, 2000.

Latour, Bruno. *Reassembling the Social: An Introduction to Actor-Network-Theory*. Oxford: Oxford University Press, 2005.

Lazzarato, Maurizio. "Immaterial Labor." In Paolo Virno and Michael Hardt, eds., *Radical Thought in Italy: A Potential Politics*. Minneapolis: University of Minnesota Press, 1996.

Lee, Edward A. "Computing Needs Time." *Communications of the ACM* 52 (5): 70–79 (2009). Available at http://cacm.acm.org/magazines/2009/5/24649-computing-needs-time/fulltext.

Leslie, Esther. *Walter Benjamin: Overpowering Conformism*. London: Pluto, 2000.

Link, David. "Scrambling T-R-U-T-H: Rotating Letters as a Material Form of Thought." In Siegfried Zielinski and Eckhard Fürlus, eds., *Variantology 4: On Deep Time Relations of Arts, Sciences and Technologies in the Arabic-Islamic World*, 215–266. Cologne: König, 2010.

Link, David. "There Must Be an Angel: On the Beginnings of the Arithmetics of Rays." In Siegfried Zielinski and David Link, eds., *Variantology 2. On Deep Time Relations of Arts, Sciences and Technologies*, 15–42. Cologne: König, 2006.

Lukács, Georg. *History and Class Consciousness: Studies in Marxism*. 1922; Cambridge, MA: MIT Press, 1976.

Mackenzie, Adrian. *Cutting Code: Software and Sociality*. New York: Peter Lang, 2006.

Malik, Shiv. "Facebook Accused of Removing Activists' Pages." *Guardian*, 29 April 2011. Available at http://www.guardian.co.uk/technology/2011/apr/29/facebook-accused-removing-activists-pages.

Marazzi, Christian. *Capital and Language: From the New Economy to the War Economy.* Trans. Gregory Conti. Los Angeles: Semiotext(e), 2008.

Marino, Mark C. "Critical Code Studies." In *Electronic Book Review* (2006). Available at http://www.electronicbookreview.com/thread/electropoetics/codology.

Marx, Karl. *Capital.* Vol. 1. Trans. Ben Fowkes. Harmondsworth: Penguin, 1990.

Marx, Karl. *Grundrisse: Foundations of the Critique of Political Economy (Rough Draft).* Harmondsworth: Penguin, 1981.

Mauss, Marcel. *The Gift: Forms and Functions of Exchange in Archaic Societies.* Trans. Ian Cunnison. London: Cohen and West, 1970.

McLean, Alex. "Artist-Programmers and Programming Languages for the Arts." PhD thesis, Goldsmiths, University of London, October 2011.

McLean, Alex, and Geraint Wiggins. "Words, Movement and Timbre." Paper delivered at NIME09 conference, Pittsburgh, 3–6 June 2009. Available at http://doc.gold.ac.uk/~ma503am/writing/nime09.pdf.

Negri, Antonio. *Marx beyond Marx: Lessons on the Grundrisse.* Ed. Jim Fleming. Trans. Harry Cleaver, Michael Ryan, and Maurizio Viano. New York: Autonomedia, 1991.

Neumark, Norie, Ross Gibson, and Theo van Leeuwen, eds. *Voice: Vocal Aesthetics in Digital Arts and Media.* Cambridge, MA: MIT Press, 2010.

Ong, Walter J. *Orality and Literacy: The Technologizing of the Word.* 1982; London: Routledge, 2002.

Poe, Edgar Allan. *The Complete Tales and Poems of Edgar Allan Poe.* New York: Vintage, 1975.

Preston, John, and Mark Bishop, eds. *Views into the Chinese Room: New Essays on Searle and Artificial Intelligence.* Oxford: Clarendon Press, 2002.

Rancière, Jacques. "Ten Theses on Politics." *Theory and Event* 5 (3) (2001). Available at http://www.egs.edu/faculty/jacques-ranciere/articles/ten-thesis-on-politics.

Raymond, Eric S. *The Art of UNIX Programming.* Boston: Addison-Wesley, 2004.

Rée, Jonathan. *I See a Voice: Language, Deafness and the Senses—A Philosophical History.* London: HarperCollins, 1999.

Roberts, John, ed. *Art Has No History! The Making and Unmaking of Modern Art.* London: Verso, 1994.

Rossiter, Ned. *Organized Networks: Media Theory, Creative Labour, New Institutions.* Rotterdam: NAi, in association with the Institute of Network Cultures, 2006.

Rushkoff, Douglas. *Program or Be Programmed: Ten Commands for a Digital Age.* Berkeley, CA: Soft Skull Press, 2011.

Schmitt, Carl. *The Concept of the Political*. 1927; Chicago: University of Chicago Press, 1996.

Scholz, Trebor. "On MTurk, Some Examples of Exploitation" (2009). Available at http://www.collectivate_net/journalisms.

Schwitters, Kurt. *Poems, Performance Pieces, Proses, Plays, Poetics*. Ed. and trans. Jerome Rothenberg and Pierre Joris. Cambridge, MA: Exact Change, 2002.

Searle, John R. "Minds, Brains, and Programs." *Behavioral and Brain Sciences* 3 (1980): 417–424.

Sondheim, Alan. "Introduction to Codework." *American Book Review* 22 (6) (September/October 2001). Available at http://www.litline.org/ABR/issues/Volume22/Issue6/sondheim.pdf.

Stallman, Richard M. *Free Software, Free Society: Selected Essays of Richard M. Stallman*. Ed. Joshua Gay. Boston: GNU Press, 2002.

Stallman, Richard M. "Why Software Should Not Have Owners." 1994. Available at http://www.gnu.org/philosophy/why-free.html.

Stephenson, Neal. *Cryptonomicon*. New York: HarperCollins, 2002.

Terranova, Tiziana. "Free Labor: Producing Culture for the Digital Economy." *Social Text* 18 (2) (2000): 33–58.

Terranova, Tiziana. *Network Culture: Politics for the Information Age*. London: Pluto Press, 2004.

Tronti, Mario. "The Strategy of Refusal" (1965). In "Autonomia: Post-political Politics," *Semiotext(e)* 3 (3) (1980): 28–34.

Virno, Paolo. *A Grammar of the Multitude: For an Analysis of Contemporary Forms of Life*. Trans. Isabella Bertoletti, James Cascaito, and Andrea Casson. New York: Semiotext(e), 2004.

Virno, Paolo. *Multitude: Between Innovation and Negation*. Trans. Isabella Bertoletti, James Cascaito, and Andrea Casson. Los Angeles: Semiotext(e), 2008.

Virno, Paolo, and Michael Hardt, eds. *Radical Thought in Italy*. Minneapolis: University of Minnesota Press, 1996.

Wall, Larry. *Programming Perl*. Sebastopol, CA: O'Reilly, 2001.

Wardrip-Fruin, Noah, and Nick Montfort, eds. *The New Media Reader*. Cambridge, MA: MIT Press, 2003.

Wiener, Norbert. *Cybernetics: or, Control and Communication in the Animal and the Machine*. 1948; Cambridge, MA: MIT Press, 1965.

Wiener, Norbert. *God and Golem, Inc.* Cambridge, MA: MIT Press, 1964.

Winogrand, Terry, and Fernando Flores. *Understanding Computers and Cognition: A New Foundation for Design*. Reading, MA: Addison-Wesley, 1987.

Wood, Gaby. *Living Dolls*. London: Faber and Faber, 2002.

Wray, Richard. "EU Says Internet Could Fall Apart." *Guardian*, 12 October 2005. Available at http://www.guardian.co.uk/business/2005/oct/12/newmedia.media.

XXXXX. Berlin and London: Openmute, 2006.

Yuill, Simon. "All Problems of Notation Will Be Solved by the Masses." *Mute* (February 2008). Available at http://www.metamute.org/en/All-Problems-of-Notation-Will-be-Solved-by -the-Masses.

Žižek, Slavoj. "Hegel's 'Logic of Essence' as a Theory of Ideology." In *The Žižek Reader*, ed. Elizabeth Wright and Edmond Wright. Oxford: Blackwell, 1999.

Žižek, Slavoj, ed. *Mapping Ideology*. London: Verso, 1997.

Žižek, Slavoj. *The Ticklish Subject: The Absent Centre of Political Ontology*. London: Verso, 1999.

Žižek, Slavoj. *Violence*. London: Profile Books, 2008.

Index